THE
POWER
OF THE
GOSPEL

An **Inductive Overview** of the **Book of Romans**

Romans

...a servant of Christ Jesus, called to
...apostle and set apart for the gos-
...the gospel he promised
...through his prophets in the
...regarding his Son, who as
...nature was a descendant of
...through the Spirit of holi-
...with power to be the Son
...rection from the dead;
...Through him and
...received grace and
...among all

to you some spiritual gift to m...
strong— ¹²that is, that you and ...
mutually encouraged by each ot...
¹³I do not want you to be unaw...
ers, that I planned many time...
you (but have been prevented ...
until now) in order that I m...
vest among you, just as ...
the other Gentiles.
¹⁴I am obligated b...
Greeks, both to ...
¹⁵That is why ...

SALLY VAN WICK

Published by Sally Van Wick
Temecula, California, U.S.A.
Printed in the U.S.A.

Cover design: HeyerVision and InsideOut Creative Arts
Interior design: InsideOut CreativeArts

For additional information please visit http://sallyvanwick.com, e-mail sally@ccbf.net, or write to 34180 Rancho California Road, Temecula, CA 92591, U.S.A.

MORE BOOKS FROM SALLY VAN WICK:

Touched and Transformed: Hope for the Hurting
A Nine-Week Discipleship Study

Toque transformador: Esperanza para los heridos
Un curso de discipulado de nueve semanas

Contents

Preface

In 1996 the Lord opened the door for my husband, Clark, and me to start a home Bible study. We were a small group of people meeting to study the Word and share Christ's love with one another. Within a year, this study became Calvary Chapel Bible Fellowship. Shortly thereafter we purchased property in Temecula wine country, where the congregation meets today and where I am currently the director of women's ministries.

In addition to writing Bible studies, I teach the women's weekly Bible study at Calvary Chapel Bible Fellowship. Although I do not consider myself a writer, I am passionate about the Word of God and consider it a privileged calling to teach women how to study the Bible and grow in the grace and knowledge of the Lord Jesus Christ, always pointing others to Jesus.

Not long ago I taught an inductive Bible study on the book of Romans, because Romans is such a foundational book for our Christian walk. The grace of God is often greatly misunderstood and cheapened by the way some live in the name of Jesus, so much so that many Christians walk around in grave clothes, having little to no power over sin. But once we understand that the grace of God is not only for salvation unto eternal life but also the resource we need for daily living, our everyday lives can go from defeat to victory.

God's grace teaches and empowers us to say no to sin. Romans teaches us that God has given us His grace for obedience to the faith. It teaches us that the moment we receive Jesus as Lord and Savior, we are justified by faith, which brings us peace with God in an upside-down world! Romans is a book of grace, showing us that the gospel is the power of God unto salvation and that nothing can separate us from the love of God that is in Christ Jesus our Lord!

This book, *The Power of the Gospel*, was written as a companion to the study we did at Calvary Chapel Bible Fellowship. It is intended for use by individual women or women's groups. While the twenty lessons in this book (two introductory studies and eighteen inductive lessons) can be done without watching the teaching, you will get the most out of this book if you watch the teaching on video in conjunction with each lesson. You can find the videos by going to sallyvanwick.com/resources/teachings and clicking on "The Book of Romans."

Through our study of Romans, I have seen lives transformed and women freed from thinking that they have to *perform* to please God. I pray that this study impresses His loving grace on your life and stirs in you a desire to know Christ more as you grow in His grace and knowledge—and are strengthened to live in and by the power of His gospel!

Special Thanks

I am so thankful to Jesus Christ for saving me and giving me a desire to study His Word so that I can know Him more, all by His extraordinary grace. He took me from a life of sin and destruction and showed me His loving-kindness that leads to repentance, touching me with the power of His Holy Spirit and forever transformed my life through His love, comfort, healing, and restoration as only He can do.

I want to give a special thanks to all who serve in the women's ministry leadership at Calvary Chapel Bible Fellowship and gave insight and inspiration through prayer and encouragement as I wrote this study on the book of Romans. Thank you, Lori Wear, Kim Thompson, and Emily Barton, for helping with the initial edit and organization.

To my editor, Becky English, thank you; it was a pleasure working with you. I definitely could not have done this without you! Bob Heyer and Rob Williams, thank you for the beautiful cover and interior designs. And Jennifer Cullis, your careful proofreading is greatly appreciated.

I especially want to thank my husband, best friend, and pastor, who is an incredible teacher of the Word and has mentored me in the grace of God.

How to Study the Bible

*As it is written: "Eye has not seen, nor ear heard, nor have entered into
the heart of man the things which God has prepared for those who love Him."
But God has revealed them to us through His Spirit. For the Spirit searches
all things, yes, the deep things of God.*

1 CORINTHIANS 2:9–10

I love to meditate on the names of God, learning more about His character and promises. Yet in Psalm 138:2 the psalmist says of God, "You have magnified Your word above all Your name." The importance of growing in our knowledge of the Word of God cannot be understated, for it is the Word that contains all we need to know about who God is so we might be transformed into His image. Peter encourages us to "grow in the grace and knowledge of our Lord and Savior Jesus Christ" (2 Pet. 3:18), and God has given us His precious Word to help us do just that. As the psalmist says in Psalm 119:114, "You are my hiding place and my shield; I hope in Your Word."

Studying God's Word is one of the most exciting things that we as Christians can do. Oh, the simplicity yet depth of the treasure of God's Word! The goal of studying the Word is to know God more intimately, not so we can be puffed up with head knowledge but so we can understand God's truth in our lives and in turn apply it daily to our lives in order to glorify His name.

The most intriguing thing about studying God's Word is that it is the Holy Spirit who teaches us what it means and brings all things to our remembrance (see John 14:26). It is God, through His Spirit, who speaks to our hearts and teaches us; it is not our intellect or our own ability to understand that makes Scripture come alive. As 1 Corinthians 2:14 states, "The natural man does not receive the things of the Spirit of God, for they are foolishness to him; nor can he know them, because they are spiritually discerned."

> The righteousness of God apart from the law is revealed, . . . even the righteousness of God, through faith in Jesus Christ, to all and on all who believe.
>
> ROMANS 3:21-22

There is no richer reward than the abiding presence of God in our lives as we seek to know Him more. Take a moment to thank Him for the gift of His Holy Spirit and for what He will teach you as you examine the book of Romans through this study tool, *The Power of the Gospel*.

Inductive Bible Study Simplified

This book approaches the book of Romans with what is called inductive Bible study. Inductive Bible study is about finding the meaning of a verse or a passage by looking at the big picture of Scripture. In other words, it means looking at the passage we are studying in context and comparing the passage to other scriptures within the Bible. This enables us to conclude the author's meaning more clearly and thoroughly.

As you study God's Word through this book, some simple guidelines may help you glean more of what the Spirit desires to teach you. Of course, as we noted above, it is not about the method we use as much as the One who teaches us. But the following three basic elements of the inductive Bible study method are helpful and will hopefully, in time, become second nature to you.

First, *observation: reading to discover what the text says*. As we read a passage, it is important to observe its context—the circumstances that form the background and setting for the events, statements, or ideas presented in the passage.

When you read a portion of Scripture, ask yourself, "What does the text say?" This first step is about discovering the basic facts of who, what, where, when, why, and how. As you read through a text in one sitting, observe and record the facts that are key to understanding what is really happening or being taught. For example, ask yourself, "At the time this was written, what was the historical setting?" "What was the political setting?" "What was the social setting?" (You may need a Bible encyclopedia to answer these questions.) These types of facts will help you accurately determine what the portion of Scripture says. Avoid interpretation or application at this point; simply report the facts as you see them.

During this step in *The Power of the Gospel*, you will be asked to pull out key words and phrases that are important to the context of the passage you are studying. The key to observation is repetition—read and reread! These key words and phrases are vital for determining what the writer is trying to communicate. The following section titled "How to Complete a Chart" offers further instruction on this subject.

Second, *interpretation: reading to discover what the text means*. The second step is to read through the facts in order to understand the meaning. You might ask, "What did that event or teaching mean to the people of that time?" "What concept does it teach?" "What can I learn?" Many of the questions in this book's lessons are designed to help you discover answers and insights for interpretation.

Finally, *application: reading to discover how the text applies to you*. This last step is rich and rewarding. After you learn what God's Word says in context and what it means through proper interpretation, you will then be able to apply it effectively and powerfully to your life. This is when you allow God's Word to judge your own heart and the transforming effect of the Word of God occurs, resulting in renewed thinking and actions. Questions in this book that ask you to respond or how you can grow or change from what you have learned are directed toward application.

How to Complete a Chart

Charts are included throughout this study to help with step 1 of inductive Bible study—observation. Charts can be helpful tools to pull truths from a text to help a reader observe things he or she might not otherwise see. The charts in this book are designed to discover facts about people, key words, instructions, exhortations, key events, doctrines, or phrases.

Before completing a chart, you will need to do two things: first, read the titles at the top of each column so you will know what words or subjects to look for in the day's assigned Scripture passage; then second, read the daily passage, and look for those particular words or topics as you read. For example, if the heading of the first column is "Jesus Christ," you will read the day's text looking only for this word or its synonyms (synonyms for Jesus Christ can be "He," "Him," "Christ," "Lord," "Jesus," "Son," and sometimes "God.") Some charts will ask you instead to first read the passage and find key words and phrases—ones that are repeated or emphasized. (Some of the key words in the book of Romans are "law," "sin," "faith," "righteousness," "spirit," "flesh," "grace," "gospel," "Israel," "Jew," "works," and "justification.") Mark these words in your Bible in ways that will cause them to stand out—underlining with a red pen, circling a word, or putting a cross over a name.

When you have finished reading and marking, record your observations and discoveries in each column of the chart and, if asked, the Scripture references where you found them. If the Scripture passage tells you that Jesus did something, write out fully all that He did or accomplished or all that was associated with Him. Some may find this redundant, but it is through repetition that we remember. Finally, write a conclusion to your findings in the box at the bottom of the chart in the form of a chapter title or summary statement.

Imagine, for example, that our Scripture passage is Romans 5:1–11:

¹Therefore, having been justified by faith, we have peace with God through our Lord Jesus Christ, ²through whom also we have access by faith into this grace in which we stand, and rejoice in hope of the glory of God. ³And not only that, but we also glory in tribulations, knowing that tribulation produces perseverance; ⁴and perseverance, character; and character, hope. ⁵Now hope does not disappoint, because the love of God has been poured out in our hearts by the Holy Spirit who was given to us.

⁶For when we were still without strength, in due time Christ died for the ungodly. ⁷For scarcely for a righteous man will one die;

yet perhaps for a good man someone would even dare to die. ⁸But God demonstrates His own love toward us, in that while we were still sinners, Christ died for us. ⁹Much more then, having now been justified by His blood, we shall be saved from wrath through Him. ¹⁰For if when we were enemies we were reconciled to God through the death of His Son, much more, having been reconciled, we shall be saved by His life. ¹¹And not only that, but we also rejoice in God through our Lord Jesus Christ, through whom we have now received the reconciliation.

You would first look at the column headings on the chart to see which words to look for as you read the passage; then you would read the passage, looking specifically for the words "Jesus," "God," and "Holy Spirit." Finally, you would write your findings, along with the verses where you found them, in the columns and then write a chapter title or chapter summary statement at the bottom of the chart.

Vs.	Jesus	Vs.	God	Vs.	Holy Spirit
5:1	Our peace with God is through our Lord Jesus Christ.	5:1	We have peace with God.	5:5	The Holy Spirit is the One God used to pour out His love into our hearts.

Chapter Title or Summary Statement

How to Complete a Word Study

While charts help with step 1 of inductive Bible study (observation), word studies will help with step 2 (interpretation). This book contains word studies that will help you better understand the book of Romans.

In order to do a word study, you will need certain tools—things like Bible dictionaries, encyclopedias, and concordances. It will greatly benefit your ability to work through *The Power of the Gospel* if you invest in several of these tools before beginning this study. (In the next section a number of good resources are recommended.)

How do these tools work? They help a student of the Bible more fully understand the background and meaning of a word in order to better understand the passage in which that word is found. For example, we might want to get a better understand of the word "propitiation" in Romans 3:23–26:

> All have sinned and fall short of the glory of God, being justified freely by His grace through the redemption that is in Christ Jesus, whom God set forth as a *propitiation* by His blood, through faith, to demonstrate His righteousness, because in His forbearance God had passed over the sins that were previously committed, to demonstrate at the present time His righteousness, that He might be just and the justifier of the one who has faith in Jesus.

To do that, we would turn to our study tools. The software-based version of *Strong's Exhaustive Concordance of the Bible*, first of all, tells us that the word "propitiation" means "an expiatory (place or thing), i.e. (concretely) an atoning victim, or (specially) the lid of the Ark (in the Temple): KJV—mercy seat, propitiation."[1] It also assigns each word a number, in this case #2435, which helps us find the word more easily if we want to study it in more depth.

Another valuable tool is *The Complete Word Study Dictionary: New Testament* by Spiros Zodhiates. Zodhiates tells us that "propitiation" is

> the lid or covering of the ark of the covenant made of pure gold, on and before which the high priest was to sprinkle the blood of the expiator sacrifices on the Day of Atonement, and where the

Lord promised to meet His people (Ex. 25:17, 22; Lev. 16:2, 14, 15). Paul, by applying this name to Christ in Rom. 3:25, assures us that Christ was the true mercy seat, the reality typified by the cover on the ark of the covenant (Heb. 9:5). Therefore, it means a place of conciliation, of expiation, what the ancients called *thusiasté rion* (2379), altar or place of sacrifice. It does not refer to the expiatory sacrifices themselves. Jesus Christ is designated . . . not only as the place where the sinner deposits his sin, but He Himself is the means of expiation. He is not like the high priest of the OT whose expiation of the people was accomplished through the blood of something other than himself (Heb. 9:25). . . .

The translation "mercy seat," symbolically referring to Jesus Christ, is . . . equivalent to the Throne of Grace. . . . In Christianity, however, it is never people who take the initiative or make the sacrifice, but God Himself who, out of His great love for sinners, provided the way by which His wrath against us might be averted. Jesus shed His blood and became the way to the Father for sinners. . . .

What the Apostle Paul refers to with the word *hilasté rion* is the means of gaining the favor of God through Jesus Christ. . . . Believing and accepting the actual bodily sacrifice of Jesus Christ in shedding His blood is a spiritual exercise of man which is sufficient to satisfy the justice of God.[2]

Nelson's Illustrated Bible Dictionary has this to say:

[pro PISH ih a shun]—the atoning death of Jesus on the cross, through which He paid the penalty demanded by God because of man's sin, thus setting mankind free from sin and death. The word comes from an old English word, propitiate, which means "to appease." Thus, propitiation expresses the idea that Jesus died on the cross to pay the price for sin which a holy God demanded of man the sinner.

Although Jesus was free of sin, He took all our sins upon Himself and redeemed us from the penalty of death which our sins demanded. As the writer of 1 John declared, "He Himself is the propitiation for our sins, and not for ours only but also for the whole world" (1 John 2:2; expiation, RSV).[3]

After you have defined a word using your study tools, complete your word study by defining the word in your own language: "To me propitiation means that Jesus is my throne of grace! He is where I meet God!"

Inductive Bible Study Resources

A number of good study tools are available.

You can find some at no cost. The Blue Letter Bible, for example, offers searchable Greek, Hebrew, and English dictionaries complete with the numbering system of *Strong's Exhaustive Concordance* and many other valuable resources; it can be found at blueletterbible.org. The Online Bible's basic starter pack contains more than thirty Bible translations and other helpful materials and can be downloaded at onlinebible.net. Bible Gateway at www.biblegateway.com and Bible Hub at biblehub.com also contain many Bible translations and a great number of study helps.

Bible dictionaries, concordances, and encyclopedias are great resources to add to your personal library. The following list contains some I like to use (the first two would be helpful for completing the word studies found in this book):

* *The Complete Word Study Dictionary: Old Testament*
  by Spiros Zodhiates
* *The Complete Word Study Dictionary: New Testament*
  by Spiros Zodhiates
* *Strong's Exhaustive Concordance of the Bible*
* *Vine's Complete Expository Dictionary*
* *International Standard Bible Encyclopedia*
* *Nelson's Illustrated Bible Dictionary*
* *New Unger's Bible Dictionary*
* Other Greek and Hebrew dictionaries

Commentaries can be helpful study companions. An important note about commentaries, however: please do not use them as a primary source of study. While commentaries are helpful, they are the result of someone else's study time—the insights of other people rather than our own. We should look to them only after we have prayed and completed our own study of the Scriptures.

Our goal in Bible study is to hear from God ourselves through the power of the Holy Spirit. The Bible is God's Word written directly to each of us, and as we study the Word and record the insights that the Spirit gives us, our findings will become our own personal commentaries. What rich fellowship we then have with one another when we can share what God is doing in our lives personally.

Having said that, two good commentaries that particularly pertain to the study in this book are these:

* *The Bible Knowledge Commentary: An Exposition of the Scriptures* (available for both Old and New Testament)
* *The Gospel According to Grace: A Clear Commentary on the Book of Romans* by Chuck Smith

The Blue Letter Bible also offers various commentaries.

Finally, as mentioned in the preface of this book, the inductive teaching that *The Power of the Gospel* is based on will be a helpful resource in completing this study. Video teaching for each lesson, including this introductory one on how to study the Bible, can be found by going to sallyvanwick.com/resources/teachings and clicking on "The Book of Romans."

Heart Preparation

While we can gather our tools and become effective students, preparation of the heart is the most vital prerequisite to effectively studying the Bible.

Prayer. Before we open the Bible, we must ask God to be our teacher and guide as we seek to understand all He has to say that we might know the things God has freely given His people (see 1 Cor. 2:12). God is interested in our growth in faith, which comes by our understanding of Him. As we pray with expectancy, we can be confident that He will reveal Himself to us through His Word.

Desire. Our life in Christ is more precious than gold. However, to have a life in Christ, we must abide in Him and draw from Him. To be spiritually healthy, we must be nourished by His Word (our spiritual food). First Peter 2:2 says, "As newborn babes, desire the pure milk of the word, that you may grow thereby." Many Christians are weak and starving because they do not rely upon the Holy Spirit and personally seek God in His Word. But Jesus said, "Man shall not live by bread alone, but by every word that proceeds from the mouth of God" (Matt. 4:4).

As with any loving Father, God has much that He wants to teach us. He desires to assure, guide, warn, enlighten, and encourage us as we walk with Him. As you work through this book, stop and take a moment before each day's study to pray and ask the Lord for a desire and hunger to feast on His Word.

Commitment. King David said, "I will not offer to the Lord that which costs me nothing" (see 2 Sam. 24:24). Without doubt there is a price to pay as we commit ourselves to the study of God's Word. Other things will distract us and vie for our time, but our commitment to God must be first and foremost in our hearts. We need to realize that there is a spiritual battle raging around us, because the enemy does not want us to continue in our walk with God. As Joshua 24:15 tells us, we must continuously choose each day whom we will serve.

If you always begin your study time alone in prayer, praying that your eyes, ears, and heart will be ready to receive, and if you truly hunger after the truth of God's Word, and if you remain committed to seeking the Lord in Scripture through the challenges that come your way, you will be richly rewarded. May God bless you as you study *The Power of the Gospel*.

Background of Romans

O Lord God Almighty, not the God of the philosophers
and the wise, but the God of the prophets and apostles; and better than all,
the God and Father of our Lord Jesus Christ, may I express Thee unblamed?
They that know Thee not may call upon Thee as other than Thou art,
and so worship not Thee but a creature of their own fancy; therefore,
enlighten our minds that we may know Thee as Thou art, so that we may
perfectly love Thee and worthily praise Thee. Amen.

A. W. TOZER

Day 1: Background Study of Romans

Paul wrote Romans around AD 55–57, during his third missionary journey, as he made his way from Corinth to Jerusalem. At the time of his writing, Rome had been an empire for about three hundred years. Rome is located on the western side of the country of Italy, which is a peninsula extending into the Mediterranean Sea. The city sits between two mountain ranges and is said to be built on seven hills. Legend says that the gods Romulus and Remus, sons of Mars, founded Rome around 800 BC.

The Etruscan people ruled Rome until replaced by a republic in 500 BC. This republic grew in its influence for the next five hundred years, sometimes having a so-called divine king (Caesar) and sometimes republican rule. At the time of Christ, Rome was the dominant world power and ascribed divinity to its rulers. The Romans built many cities and were famous for their roads, which were designed to link the entire empire. By the time of Paul's writings, the Roman Empire stretched as far west as modern-day England.

Roman culture was patriarchal, with the man of the family having complete control over all aspects of his household. Women had some rights but were not permitted the highly esteemed right of citizenship. To be a Roman citizen, a man had to either serve as a lifetime legionnaire (soldier), be born of Roman citizens, be born in a certain locale (as in the case of Saul of Tarsus, as Paul was formerly called), or be adopted by a Roman citizen. Activities such as voting and owning property were reserved exclusively for citizens. Also, if accused of a crime, citizens alone were granted the right to be heard in certain courts or even before Caesar himself.

Rome had many slaves who had mostly been conquered from other lands. Some were well educated and became tutors and doctors of Roman society. Some were treated cruelly, while others were treated with kindness and even paid wages so they would have the resources with which to buy their freedom. Rome ruled all the lands it conquered dictatorially but not unreasonably, as long as those conquered were willing to worship (pay tribute both with resources and attitude) the Caesars.

Rome gave today's world several of our traditions and institutions. For instance, some of our marriage ceremony traditions are from Rome, such as wearing a wedding ring made of metal on the fourth finger of the left hand. The Romans also made good use of the concept of public libraries, and literacy was highly esteemed.

In the time of Paul, Rome was a large, crowded, dirty city. The well to do lived in spacious homes, but the general public lived in cramped apartment-style dwellings built of stone or wood, sometimes as tall as five stories. Often these buildings collapsed. Though the city of Rome had a water delivery system and a sewer system, the structures for the poor had no plumbing, and waste was poured down communal drains. Large cities like Rome had government offices, courts, libraries, temples, shops, workshops, and public bathhouses and bathrooms. They also had theaters (half circles) and amphitheaters (full circles) for entertainment, with acoustics that we envy today.

Roman "entertainment" is famous throughout history as brutal, with fights to the death between men, contests between men and wild animals, and public executions sometimes carried out by watching a wild animal tear apart and devour a "criminal." The Romans were a people of leisure and pleasure, which became the ultimate downfall of the society.

Observe, Interpret, Apply

1. Spend the rest of today's study prayerfully reading the entire book of Romans in one sitting. Don't get bogged down with detail; just look for main characters and main events. Remember, the plain things are the main things.

2. After you read, record below what stood out to you most.

Day 2: Paul's Readers and Companions

Begin your study today by spending a few moments in prayer, asking the Holy Spirit to open the eyes of your understanding while you are studying.

Observe, Interpret, Apply

1. According to Romans 1:7, to whom did Paul write in Rome?

2. Romans 16:1–2 and 16:21–23 name Paul's companions, or helpers, at the time he wrote Romans. List these people below.

3. During Paul's time, two Jewish sects were actively perverting the gospel in Rome. First, those who were anti-law were called Antinomians. They taught that man could live any way he wanted, since he was saved by God's grace and could do nothing to earn his salvation. Their thinking was that the more a person sinned, the more grace had opportunity to show itself. Then there were the Judaizers, known as the legalists of the day. They added to the grace of God by believing people had to keep the Jewish law and traditions, including circumcision. Understanding these sects and their teachings helps us understand what Paul was dealing with and his purpose for writing the book of Romans.

In your own words, summarize Paul's purpose in writing to the saints at Rome as stated in Romans 1:1–17 and 15:14–16:27.

....

....

....

....

....

....

Digging Deeper (Optional)
Use Bible dictionaries and encyclopedias to briefly describe what Rome was like at the time Paul wrote Romans. (You may use regular dictionaries and encyclopedias as well.)

Politically:

....

....

....

Historically:

....

....

....

Economically:

_____

_____

_____

_____

Socially:

_____

_____

_____

Day 3: Romans 1

Read Romans 1. Before you start studying, pray! Spiritual things are spiritually discerned. Ask the Lord to reveal all He has for you in this study.

Observe, Interpret, Apply
1. Read Romans 1, pulling out key words and phrases (words or ideas that are repeated or key to the context). Then title each passage at the bottom of the chart.

Vs.	Romans 1:1-7	Vs.	Romans 1:8-17	Vs.	Romans 1:18-32

Vs. Romans 1:1–7	Vs. Romans 1:8–17	Vs. Romans 1:18–32
Passage Title	**Passage Title**	**Passage Title**

Hint: some of the key words are "called," "gospel," "truth," "holy Scriptures," "wrath," "righteousness," "unrighteousness," "Jesus Christ," "Son," "God," "faith," and "grace."

2. Below are listed a few key people in the book of Romans. Read Romans 1 again, and write down all the things you see pertaining to each person or group of people here.

Paul:

_____

_____

_____

_____

Saints:

_____

_____

_____

_____

Ungodly men:

_____

_____

_____

_____

_____

_____

_____

3. What does it mean that "the just shall live by faith"?

_____

_____

_____

_____

> This Good News tells us that God makes us ready for heaven—makes us right in God's sight—when we put our faith and trust in Christ to save us. This is accomplished from start to finish by faith. As the Scripture says it, "The man who finds life will find it through trusting God."
>
> ROMANS 1:17, TLB

4. Define "just" using your study tools (Strong's #1342), and write its meaning below.

_____

_____

_____

_____

_____

_____

Day 4: A Bondservant

We are all very busy. We run from place to place, living fast-paced lives; quiet times are a rarity for most of us.

Don't allow yourself to study in rote fashion, trying to take in "fast food." The Word of God is living, active, and powerful! Stop and pray, allowing the Spirit to make the Word of God alive in your heart today. Sit at His feet and ask Him to minister to you through your study.

Observe, Interpret, Apply

1. Paul identifies himself as a bondservant of Jesus Christ. Using your study tools, define the word "bondservant" (Strong's #1401), and write its meaning below.

2. To gain an Old Testament picture of a slave who lovingly and willfully binds himself to his master, read Exodus 21:2–6. Describe such a person below.

3. How do today's piercings differ from the piercing we see in Exodus 21?

4. Describe how you think a bondservant of Jesus would look today.

5. As a believer, you are called to serve the body of Christ. Are you serving Christ as a willing bondservant? Why or why not?

6. What does 2 Corinthians 9:12–15 say about this type of serving?

7. When you are a bondservant of Jesus, what is displayed? (See 2 Cor. 9:14.)

8. What attribute of God does He wish to see in the lives of His children, according to 1 John 4:12–13?

9. God isn't interested in the outward appearance of a person; what is He looking for? (See 1 Sam. 16:7.)

> Has the LORD as great delight in burnt offerings and sacrifices, as in obeying the voice of the LORD? Behold, to obey is better than sacrifice, and to heed than the fat of rams. For rebellion is as the sin of witchcraft, and stubbornness is as iniquity and idolatry.
>
> 1 SAMUEL 15:22–23

10. Have you been guilty of looking at the outward appearance of others? If so, take it to the Lord in prayer and ask Him to give you His love for others.

11. Look up Romans 1:5. What provision does God give us to enable us to be bondservants?

12. How does Hebrews 12:28–29 support this concept from Romans 1:5?

13. Note that "it is God who works in you to both will and to do for His good pleasure" (Phil. 2:13). Stop and thank Him for the work He is doing in and through you by His Spirit. Thank Him for His provision of grace.

Day 5: Paul's Purpose in Writing Romans

As we have seen, Paul had several reasons for writing the book of Romans. Today we will review those as we prepare to launch into our study of this book.

Observe, Interpret, Apply

1. List five basic reasons Paul wrote the book of Romans as stated in Romans 1:11–15.

2. In Romans 1:12 Paul says that one of his reasons for writing Romans was so that both he and his readers would be "encouraged together" by "mutual faith." How does fellowship with others who share a mutual faith encourage you?

3. What are some benefits of the saints assembling together as listed in Hebrews 10:24–25?

4. Paul understood the importance of knowing the difference between law and grace. Using your Bible and study tools (concordance and Bible dictionary), look up the definitions of "law" and "grace," and record your findings, along with any additional scriptures you can find on these topics, in

the top boxes of the chart. Then, in the bottom boxes, mark the contrasts between the two.

Law (Strong's #3551)	Grace (Strong's #5485)
Galatians 3:24	Titus 2:11–13
2 Corinthians 3:6	
Contrast Between Law and Grace	

5. List six specific promises God made to Israel in Jeremiah 32:38–40.

6. According to Jeremiah 32:40, how long will God's new covenant of grace remain in effect?

7. Hebrews 8:13 states, "In that He says, 'A new covenant,' He has made the first obsolete." The old covenant (the law) was a blood covenant, a covenant of the blood of bulls and goats. How does Jesus describe the new covenant in Matthew 26:28–29?

8. What does Hebrews 10:4 say about the old covenant?

9. Stop and thank God that you are no longer under law but now have a new covenant of grace. Write your thanks below.

10. Go back over this week's lesson, and highlight the scripture or concept that ministered to you the most. Write why it spoke to you below.

....

....

....

....

....

Romans at a Glance

God's Righteousness	Chapter	Subject
For sinners	1	Gentiles
	2	Jews
	3	All have sinned
For the saved	3	Righteousness through redemption
	4	Righteousness through imputation
	5	Through reconciliation
For the sanctified	6	Believers dead to sin
	7	Believers dead to law
	8	Living by the Spirit
By God's sovereignty	9	God's election, or choice
	10	Man's free will to believe
	11	Gentiles grafted in
For God's service	12	Worship's spiritual service
	13	Rendering what is due
	14	Not judging others' convictions
	15	Accepting/loving one another
	16	Rejecting the false and obeying the truth

Romans 1:1–17

Lord, teach me to listen. The times are noisy and my ears are weary with the thousand raucous sounds, which continuously assault them. Give me the spirit of the boy Samuel when he said to Thee, "Speak, for Thy servant heareth." Let me hear Thee speaking in my heart. Let me get used to the sound of Thy Voice, that its tones may be familiar when the sounds of earth die away and the only sound will be the music of Thy speaking Voice. Amen!

A. W. TOZER

Day 1: Paul the Apostle

A Jew born in Tarsus of Cilicia, Saul lived as a Pharisee and studied under Gamaliel. He was also a citizen of Rome. Paul, as he was later called, referred to himself in his early days as a zealous Jew: "You have heard of my former conduct in Judaism, how I persecuted the church of God beyond measure and tried to destroy it. And I advanced in Judaism beyond many of my contemporaries in my own nation, being more exceedingly zealous for the traditions of my fathers" (Gal. 1:13–14).

Saul's zeal for the Lord and his standing in the Jewish religious community gave him the authority to arrest Christians, imprisoning many and approving of their deaths. In fact, he attended and consented to the stoning of the first martyr, Stephen (see Acts 7:58; 8:3). Later in his life he recorded his journey to Damascus to seize Christians and put them in prison: "Suddenly a great light from heaven shone around me. And I fell to the ground and heard a voice saying to me, 'Saul, Saul, why are you persecuting Me?' So I answered, 'Who are You, Lord?' And He said to me, 'I am Jesus of Nazareth, whom you are persecuting'" (Acts 22:6–8). Another account of Saul's conversion is found in Acts 9.

After his conversion Saul received a new name from God—he would now be called Paul (see Acts 13:9). Instead of being taught about the gospel by men, Paul went to Arabia for three years and was given the gospel by direct revelation from Jesus before returning to Damascus.

Paul then went to Jerusalem, where he stayed with Peter for fifteen days. Afterward he went to Syria and Cilicia and preached the gospel. Fourteen years later Paul went up to Jerusalem with Barnabas and Titus (see Gal. 1–2). He preached the gospel in Damascus, then in Jerusalem and Judea, and then to the Gentiles, according to Acts 26:20. Paul considered himself an apostle to the Gentiles (see Rom. 11:13). Acts 13:1–21:1 indicates that Paul completed three missionary journeys. Some believe that Paul made a fourth missionary journey to Spain (see Rom. 15:24, 28). Clement of Rome indicates that Paul took the gospel to Spain before returning to Rome.

The apostle Paul was given a "thorn in the flesh," which he prayed three times for God to remove: "Lest I should be exalted above measure by the abundance of the revelations, a thorn in the flesh was given to me, a messenger of Satan to buffet me" (2 Cor. 12:7). Some believe his eyes were afflicted, due to the nature of his conversion, but the Bible does not state specifically what Paul's "thorn" was. Although God used Paul to heal others, Paul himself was not healed.

In 2 Corinthians 11:23–27 Paul describes the many trials and tribulations he experienced during his ministry and testimony for the Lord Jesus Christ:

In labors more abundant, in stripes above measure, in prisons more frequently, in deaths often. From the Jews five times I received forty stripes minus one. Three times I was beaten with rods; once I was stoned; three times I was shipwrecked; a night and a day I have been in the deep; in journeys often, in perils of waters, in perils of robbers, in perils of my own countrymen, in perils of the Gentiles, in perils in the city, in perils in the wilderness, in perils in the sea, in perils among false brethren; in weariness and toil, in sleeplessness often, in hunger and thirst, in fastings often, in cold and nakedness.

Paul was imprisoned in Rome twice. His final imprisonment was in AD 67 following his return from Spain, and he was beheaded in AD 67 or 68 during the reign of Caesar Nero.

Through all Paul's trials, he rejoiced as he focused upon his great God and Savior Jesus Christ:

Oh, the depth of the riches both of the wisdom and knowledge of God! How unsearchable are His judgments and His ways past finding out! "For who has known the mind of the LORD? Or who has become His counselor?" "Or who has first given to Him and it shall be repaid to him?" For of Him and through Him and to Him are all things, to whom be glory forever. Amen. (Rom. 11:33–36)

One result of Paul's focus on the Lord is the rich trove of letters he wrote to the churches of his day that came to form a large part of the New Testament. Below are listed some of Paul's writings.

Decade	Book	Place Written	Dates Written
AD 50-59	1 and 2 Thessalonians	Corinth	AD 50-54, during Paul's second missionary journey
	1 Corinthians	Ephesus	AD 56, during Paul's third missionary journey
	2 Corinthians	Macedonia	AD 56, during Paul's third missionary journey
	Romans	Corinth	AD 57, during Paul's third missionary journey
AD 60-69	Ephesians	Rome	AD 60, during Paul's fourth missionary journey
	Philippians	Rome	AD 60-61
	Colossians	Rome	AD 60-62
	Philemon	Rome	AD 60-62

Only the servants of truth can ever know truth. You can fill your head full of knowledge but the day you decide that you are going to obey God, it will get down into your heart. He will illuminate your spirit, and the truth you have known will then be known spiritually, and power will begin to flow up and out and you will find yourself marvelously changed forever.

A. W. TOZER

Observe, Interpret, Apply

1. What is one thing that stands out in your mind regarding Paul's background?

2. Paul describes himself as a bondservant. How does that inspire you?

3. Are you willing to call yourself a bondservant of Jesus Christ?

Day 2: Romans 1:1–7

Prayerfully read Romans 1:1–7.

Observe, Interpret, Apply

1. What do you think Paul meant when he said in verse 1 that he was "called to be an apostle, *separated* to the gospel of God"?

2. Using your study tools, define the word "separated" (Strong's #873), and write its meaning below.

3. Why would we want to be sanctified? Look up 1 Thessalonians 4:3–5 to help you answer.

4. Write out Titus 2:11–14. Meditate on this verse, memorizing it if you can. What provision does God give to us so we can be separated to the gospel?

5. When is it acceptable to partake in worldly activities to gain favor with those with whom we desire to share the gospel? Look up 2 Corinthians 6:17–18 to help you answer.

6. Read Galatians 1:15–16. What was God's plan for Paul?

7. Do you believe that God has a plan for your life? If so, what is it?

8. In Romans 1:3–4 Paul describes Jesus as the Son of God. How does John 1:14 describe Jesus?

9. Look up Hebrews 9:13–15. What does it mean to you personally that Jesus was "declared to be the Son of God with power according to the Spirit of holiness, by the resurrection from the dead" (Rom. 1:4)?

10. According to Colossians 3:1-4, where is Jesus right now?

11. Where are we as believers in Jesus, according to Ephesians 2:4-7? (Note particularly verse 6.)

12. Look up Colossians 1:26-27. According to this passage, what is our hope?

13. Write out Romans 1:5 and then underline the provision God has given "for obedience to the faith."

14. Define "grace" using your study tools (Strong's #5485), and write its meaning below.

15. To whom does God give grace, according to James 4:6 and 1 Peter 5:5?

16. How do we access grace, according to Romans 5:1–2?

17. Define the word "apostleship" using your study tools (Strong's #651), and write its meaning below.

18. Make apostleship personal by commenting on what Paul says to the church in 2 Corinthians 5:20–21. What does this passage say to you?

19. Notice that Paul says in Romans 1:5 that we have "received" rather than earned. How does Ephesians 2:8–10 confirm this concept?

20. Note Paul's use of the word "we" in Romans 1:5. Paul now speaks of all believers, not only himself. We all have received God's glorious grace, which means His favor, mercy, love, and divine influence upon our hearts. Grace includes all that God has done for us and all the wonderful blessings He showers upon us. Titus 2:11–14 shows us a perfect picture of this definition of grace. Review these verses, and record below a new perspective of God's grace and what it means in your life.

> Pride goes before destruction and a haughty spirit before a fall.
>
> PROVERBS 16:18

_____

_____

_____

_____

_____

_____

_____

Day 3: Romans 1:8–11

Prayerfully read Romans 1:8–11.

Observe, Interpret, Apply

1. To show his great love for the Roman believers, Paul shared with them his purpose for writing to them. He explained that he was writing because he could do nothing else; he was compelled to share the gospel with the entire world, including the capital of the world, Rome itself. List some of the things that would encourage you from Romans 1:8–11 if you were the recipient of this letter.

_____

_____

_____

THE POWER OF THE GOSPEL

2. Note that Paul was a man of intercessory prayer and prayed for his readers. The gospel moved him to pray without ceasing (see Rom. 1:9). What is intercessory prayer?

3. Using a concordance, look up other references that speak about praying without ceasing, and list below what you learn.

4. How can we pray without ceasing?

5. Write out Ephesians 3:14–21. As you let the words from this passage bless you, think of someone in your life for whom you can intercede, and replace the word "you" in the scripture with that person's name.

Day 4: Romans 1:12–15

Prayerfully read Romans 1:12–15.

Observe, Interpret, Apply

1. Using your study tools, look up the word "encouraged" from Romans 1:12 (Strong's #4837), and write its definition below.

2. Share a time you have been encouraged or comforted by another Christian.

> If you want that splendid power in prayer, you must remain in loving, living, lasting, conscious, practical, abiding union with the Lord Jesus Christ.
>
> C. H. SPURGEON

3. What is the "mutual faith" Paul talks about in Romans 1:12?

4. Look up Ephesians 4:4–6 for a further understanding of this "mutual faith" (Rom. 1:12), and record your findings below.

5. How can you apply Hebrews 10:23–25 to this study?

_____

_____

_____

_____

> Gathering together with God's people has a two-way effect. You cannot minister to others without being ministered to yourself. Sowing the truth in love always reaps the same! That's the beauty of sharing our spiritual gifts with one another.
>
> PASTOR CHUCK SMITH

6. What could hinder us from coming together, according to the following verses?

1 Thessalonians 2:18:

_____

_____

_____

Acts 16:7:

_____

_____

7. How are we able to discern which one in the question above may be hindering us?

_____

_____

_____

_____

_____

8. What did Paul mean when he wrote, "I am a debtor both to Greeks and to barbarians, both to wise and to unwise" (Rom. 1:14)?

_____

_____

_____

_____

9. Paul felt an obligation to all men, as we also should. What does this tell you about Paul's heart?

10. In Romans 1:15 Paul wrote that he was ready to visit the church in Rome. Look up the following references, and note what they say about being ready.

2 Timothy 4:2:

1 Peter 3:15:

11. What do you think would motivate a heart to be ready?

Day 5: Romans 1:16–17

Prayerfully read Romans 1:16–17.

Observe, Interpret, Apply

1. Paul ached to share the gospel. He preached Jesus everywhere he went so that people could believe. Are you aching to share the gospel with others? What gives a person that desire?

2. What does Paul proclaim in Romans 1:16? Write it out here.

3. Persecution was on the rise when Paul wrote to Timothy in 2 Timothy 1. Young Timothy was not ashamed, but there was a possibility he could become ashamed as persecution increased. So too today, with persecution on the rise and Christianity offensive to so many, it may be easy for you to become ashamed. Record below what Paul wrote in 2 Timothy 1:8–12. Take this to heart, as this message is needed as much today as it was back then.

4. What has God given you so that you need not be ashamed of the gospel, according to 2 Timothy 1:6–7?

5. What is the gospel, according to Romans 1:16?

6. Can you remember a time when you were ashamed or embarrassed to share the gospel? God has not given you a spirit of fear. Pray and ask God to fill you with the boldness of His Spirit to speak life into the lost. The gospel is the power of God unto salvation for all!

> Whoever is ashamed of Me and My words in this adulterous and sinful generation, of him the Son of Man also will be ashamed when He comes in the glory of His Father with the holy angels.
>
> MARK 8:38

7. Look up Psalm 25:1–5. Allow this to be your prayer today.

8. The main theme of the book of Romans is the righteousness of God, as seen in Romans 1:16–17. Look up the word "righteousness" (Strong's #1343) with your study tools, and write out the definition below.

9. How is the righteousness of God revealed?

10. How do we obtain the righteousness of God?

11. What does Galatians 2:21 say about righteousness?

12. How is our faith increased, according to the following verses?

> He made Him who
> knew no sin to be sin
> for us, that we might
> become the righteousness
> of God in Him.
>
> 2 CORINTHIANS 5:21

Romans 1:17:

Romans 10:17:

Galatians 3:11:

_____

_____

13. Reread Romans 1:1–17. Is there an exhortation or an encouragement in it for you as a believer in Jesus Christ?

_____

_____

_____

_____

14. Is there an example in Romans 1:1–17 for you to follow?

_____

_____

_____

_____

15. Did you gain any fresh insights this week as you studied the Word?

_____

_____

_____

Trust in the LORD with all your heart, and lean not on your own understanding; in all your ways acknowledge Him, and He shall direct your paths.

PROVERBS 3:5–6

Sing to the LORD, bless His name; proclaim the good news of His salvation from day to day. Declare His glory among the nations, His wonders among all peoples.

PSALM 96:2–3

Romans 1:18–32

Lord, how great is our dilemma! In Thy Presence silence best becomes us, but love inflames our hearts and constrains us to speak. Were we to hold our peace the stones would cry out; yet if we speak what shall we say? Teach us to know that we cannot know, for the things of God knoweth no man, but the Spirit of God. Let faith support us where reason fails, and we shall think because we believe, not in order that we may believe. In Jesus' name. Amen.

A. W. TOZER

Day 1: Overview of Romans 1:1–32

Today we will briefly review last week's passage, Romans 1:1–17, as well as begin looking at this week's passage, Romans 1:18–32. Spend a few moments in prayer asking God to reveal all He has for you today.

Observe, Interpret, Apply

1. Write out Romans 1:16–17 as a reminder to you of the importance of the gospel and our calling to be ambassadors for Christ.

2. What stood out to you most from last week's lesson?

3. Remember to read Scripture with a purpose as you begin this new section. Allow the passage to be fresh each time you read it, asking yourself who, what, where, when, why, and how. Don't get discouraged with the repetition. This is how we hide the Word of God in our hearts that we might not sin against Him (see Ps. 119:11). Read all of Romans 1; then write key words and phrases in the chart below, and give each passage a title.

Romans 1:1-17	Romans 1:18-32

Passage Title	Passage Title

4. List reasons why God would need to impute His righteousness to us. Use Jeremiah 17:9-10 to help you answer.

_____

_____

_____

_____

5. Until we understand that the purpose of the law is to point us to Christ and His provision, we will continue to work for our salvation and sanctification. Oh, how futile it is to work to obtain that which only Jesus can provide! When we fail to understand that we can do nothing to earn God's favor, we live in constant defeat (see 2 Cor. 3:5-6). How does Titus 3:5-8 encourage you in this regard today?

_____

_____

_____

_____

Day 2: Romans 1:18–20

Prayerfully read Romans 1:18–20.

Observe, Interpret, Apply

1. Romans 1:18 says that "the wrath of God is revealed from heaven against all ungodliness and unrighteousness of men, who suppress the truth in unrighteousness." Define the words in the chart below; also list some biblical examples of the use of each word if you can.

"Ungodliness" (Strong's #763)	"Unrighteousness" (Strong's #93)	"Debased" (from Rom. 8:28, Strong's #96)

2. Some view Romans 1:18 as harsh and unfair. What does Deuteronomy 32:3-4 say about God's character?

_____

_____

_____

_____

3. Wickedness is contrary to the righteousness of God. Read the first part of Habakkuk 1:13, and comment. Note that the phrase "look on" means "to embrace."

_____

_____

_____

_____

The LORD's hand is not shortened, that it cannot save; nor His ear heavy, that it cannot hear. But your iniquities have separated you from your God; and your sins have hidden His face from you, so that He will not hear.

ISAIAH 59:1-2

4. In Genesis we see that, from the very beginning, man was created to enjoy perfect communion (unhindered fellowship) with God. According to Isaiah 59:1-2, it was not God who broke that fellowship but man. Sin entered the world through Adam and Eve, and ever since the fall in the garden, we all struggle with sin. Because of His great love for us, however, God has given us the ability to choose to follow Him in truth or fall into the deception of the enemy. God always has and always will make Himself known to all! This is why the Bible says that there is none without excuse. What does Romans 1:19-20 say to support this?

_____

_____

_____

_____

The heavens declare the glory of God; and the firmament shows His handiwork. Day unto day utters speech, and night unto night reveals knowledge.

PSALM 19:1-2

5. What about those who live in remote areas and have never been presented with the gospel? Can they be saved? Look up the following verses, and comment.

Romans 2:15-16:

John 1:9-11:

6. While we are called to tell people about Jesus, is it valid for us to worry about people who have not heard the actual name of Jesus? Why or why not? Explain your answer using the Scriptures. (Use Hebrews 7:25 and 2 Peter 3:9, among other verses, to help support your answer.)

Day 3: Romans 1:21–31

Prayerfully read Romans 1:21-31.

Observe, Interpret, Apply

1. Having read Romans 1:21-31, comment below on what you see.

_____

_____

_____

_____

_____

2. Romans 1:21 says, "Although they knew God, they did not glorify Him as God, nor were thankful, but became futile in their thoughts, and their foolish hearts were darkened." Is knowing *about* God enough to get you into heaven?

_____

_____

_____

_____

3. What do the following scriptures say about knowing about God?

Matthew 7:21–23:

_____

_____

James 2:19–20:

_____

_____

4. Comment in your own words what it means to know about someone.

5. What is God's desire for His people? Look up the following verses, and comment.

    1 Peter 4:11:

    1 Corinthians 10:31–33:

6. Why is it important for God's children to be thankful, according to 1 Thessalonians 5:18?

7. What causes thanksgiving in a believer's life, according to 2 Corinthians 4:15?

8. Romans 1:21 says that those who knew God did not bring glory to God nor were they thankful because "their foolish hearts were darkened." Look up the following verses, and comment.

John 3:19–21:

1 Corinthians 3:18–20:

"Not by might nor by power, but by My Spirit," says the LORD of hosts.

ZECHARIAH 4:6

9. What are some of the ways people can "dishonor their bodies among themselves," according to Romans 1:24–31? How are these ways reflected in today's society?

10. What does the phrase "in the lusts of their hearts" (Rom. 1:24) mean?

> Many people hold a prideful view of themselves, as the Pharisee who said, "God, I thank Thee that I am not as other men" (Luke 18:11). They feel smug because they're innocent of some of the grosser forms of sin. Yet they go to a movie or watch a TV program as actors portray these vile things, and they actually enjoy or "have pleasure in them that do them." We need to take great care not to sow to our flesh in any way. "For he that soweth to his flesh shall of the flesh reap corruption" (Galatians 6:8).
>
> PASTOR CHUCK SMITH

11. Many times we view sin on a scale, thinking that the sins listed in Romans 1 are the greatest of all sins. But in God's eyes all sin is equal; all sin is a transgression against God's law. Look up Proverbs 6:16–19, and list the seven things that are an abomination to the Lord.

12. Go back through the lists of sins in Romans 1 and Proverbs 6:16–19. Are any of the sins in these lists evident in your life? If so, pray, and ask God to cleanse your heart (see 1 John 1:9).

13. If there is a lack of repentance in our hearts, what will be the eventual result, according to Romans 1:21?

Digging Deeper (Optional)

From Romans 1:18–20, make a list of God's "invisible attributes" that are "clearly seen" and that make people "without excuse."

_____

_____

_____

_____

_____

> Righteousness exalts
> a nation, but sin is a
> reproach to any people.
>
> PROVERBS 14:34

Day 4: Romans 1:26–27

Prayerfully read Romans 1:26-27.

Observe, Interpret, Apply

1. Romans 1:26–27 states, "Even the women turned against the natural way to have sex and instead indulged in sex with each other. And the men, instead of having normal sexual relations with women, burned with lust for each other. Men did shameful things with other men" (NLT). How does Romans 1:26–27 contrast with God's design for marriage as stated in Matthew 19:4–6?

_____

_____

_____

_____

_____

_____

2. According to Romans 1:27, what is the result of not following God's design?

_____

_____

_____

_____

_____

3. Compare the result above with 1 Corinthians 6:18, and share any insights you have.

_____

_____

_____

_____

> They will perish, but You will endure; yes, they will all grow old like a garment; like a cloak You will change them, and they will be changed. But You are the same, and Your years will have no end.
>
> PSALM 102:26–27

4. At the time of Paul's writing, the Roman culture openly accepted and practiced homosexuality. Do you think God's view of marriage has changed from Paul's day to ours? Why or why not? (See 1 Peter 1:23–25 to help you answer.)

_____

_____

_____

_____

5. Compare Romans 1:26–27 with John 3:17–21. What do you see?

_____

_____

_____

_____

6. Considering your study this week, what do God's Word and the condition of our society show the need for?

_____

_____

_____

_____

7. As Christians, it is important that we know what we believe. Look up the following verses, and answer the question, "What is truth?"

Psalm 119:160:

_____

_____

_____

John 14:6:

_____

_____

John 14:17:

_____

_____

_____

John 17:17:

_____

_____

> We know that the Son of God has come and has given us an understanding, that we may know Him who is true; and we are in Him who is true, in His Son Jesus Christ. This is the true God and eternal life.
>
> 1 JOHN 5:20-21

8. Contrary to what the world would like us to think, God's Word is absolute. The current tolerance for and even celebration over ungodly and unrighteous activity is alarming, to say the least. Billy Graham has been quoted as saying, "If judgment does not fall upon America, God will owe Sodom and Gomorrah an apology." What does the Bible say about unrighteousness, according to the following verses?

Jude 1:5-7:

_____

_____

_____

_____

1 Corinthians 6:9–12 (especially verse 11):

Day 5: Review of Romans 1:18–32

Prayerfully read Romans 1:18–32.

As by one man's disobedience [Adam's] many were made sinners, so also by one Man's obedience [Jesus'] many will be made righteous. Moreover the law entered that the offense might abound. But where sin abounded, grace abounded much more, so that as sin reigned in death, even so grace might reign through righteousness to eternal life through Jesus Christ our Lord.

ROMANS 5:19–21

Observe, Interpret, Apply

1. "Retaining God in our knowledge" (see Rom. 1:28) means remembering daily what Paul says in 1 Corinthians 6:19–20: "Do you not know that your body is the temple of the Holy Spirit who is in you, whom you have from God, and you are not your own? For you were bought at a price; therefore glorify God in your body and in your spirit, which are God's." Look up Joshua 24:14–15, and summarize how we can retain God in our knowledge.

2. Personalize Joshua 24:14 as your prayer today, and write it out here.

3. Throughout his writings Paul exhorts believers to glorify God in the way they live. Look up the following scriptures, and highlight what ministers to you most.

Romans 12:1–2:

_____

_____

_____

Hebrews 10:22:

_____

_____

_____

Philippians 2:15–16:

_____

_____

You were once dark-
ness, but now you are
light in the Lord. Walk
as children of light
(for the fruit of the
Spirit is in all goodness,
righteousness, and
truth), finding out
what is acceptable
to the Lord.

EPHESIANS 5:8–10

4. Read Romans 1:32 carefully. The righteous judgment of God will be exercised on those who practice sin in a non-repentant state of disobedience to His Word. What is the penalty of such behavior?

_____

_____

_____

5. Before you are too hard on someone you know who is practicing such sins, carefully record what the second half of Romans 1:32 says. While you may not physically practice the behaviors listed in Romans 1:24–31, consider whether you approve of people who do these things, excusing their behavior, or perhaps whether you yourself might have attitudes that could make you just as guilty before God as those who actually carry out these actions. Record your thoughts below.

_____

_____

_____

_____

_____

6. What do you learn from Romans 1:18–32 regarding man's position apart from God?

> It is altogether doubtful whether any man can be saved who comes to Christ for His help but with no intention of obeying Him.
>
> A. W. TOZER

7. How are we as Christians to respond to the growing influence of homosexuality and sexual confusion in our culture? We have seen a massive shift in recent years in attitudes toward this subject, and it seems that most support and even promote the gay-transgender agenda. Any disapproval of this change has become the equivalent of racism, bigotry, hatred, and even a violation of human rights.

As believers, we must make sure that we do not overemphasize one sin over another. The Bible does not single out homosexual behavior as more sinful than drunkenness, thievery, adultery, fornication, idolatry, blasphemy, greed, hatred, or any other specific sin, and neither should we. In fact, the Bible mentions homosexuality right alongside a variety of other sins, maybe because it was as common then as it is becoming today (see Rom. 1:29–31; 1 Cor. 6:9–10; 1 Tim. 1:9–10).

> Don't you realize how patient he is being with you? Or don't you care? Can't you see that he has been waiting all this time without punishing you, to give you time to turn from your sin? His kindness is meant to lead you to repentance.
>
> ROMANS 2:4, TLB

As with every sin, sexual immorality is a *symptom* of not actively seeking after and abiding in God. We are all sinners, and all sin is equal in God's eyes; consequently, sinners are condemned to damnation apart from Christ. People end up in hell because they reject Jesus as Savior, not because they are sinners. However, the root of a sinful lifestyle is always traced back to rejecting God's plan of salvation through the sacrifice of Jesus. The fruit of this decision results in ungodliness and unrighteous living, which is the opposite of what God deems acceptable. God's way of dealing with sin is to attack it at the root, and that's how we are to deal with it as well. Therefore, regardless of people's sin, we are to approach others with their need for Jesus, always showing God's love, mercy, and compassion.

The real issue, regardless of the specific sin, is that "the wrath of God is revealed from heaven against *all* ungodliness and unrighteousness of men, who suppress the truth in unrighteousness" (Rom. 1:18). Thus, all people need the gospel of Jesus Christ. We must remember that Romans 5:8 says, "God demonstrates His own love toward *us*, in that while *we* were still sinners, Christ died for *us*."

We must not, however, confuse loving a person with condoning his or her sin. We must be careful not to partake in anyone's sin or change our biblical standard in order to share the gospel. Yes, the Bible says that homosexuality is sin, but remember, homosexuality is a secondary issue. It is a symptom of man's universal problem: being dead in trespasses and sins apart from Jesus. The only remedy is salvation, which comes through personal faith in Jesus Christ.[1]

What have you learned or seen from a new perspective in this week's lesson? Write it below.

> The end of all things is at hand; therefore be serious and watchful in your prayers. And above all things have fervent love for one another, for "love will cover a multitude of sins." Be hospitable to one another without grumbling. As each one has received a gift, minister it to one another, as good stewards of the manifold grace of God.
>
> 1 PETER 4:7-10

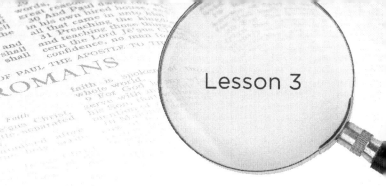
Romans 2:1–29

Our Father, we love Thee for Thy justice. We acknowledge that
Thy judgments are true and righteous altogether. Thy justice upholds the order of
the universe and guarantees the safety of all who put their trust in Thee.
We live because Thou art just and merciful. Holy, holy, holy, Lord God Almighty,
righteous in all Thy ways and holy in all Thy works. Amen.

A. W. TOZER

Day 1: Overview of Romans 2:1–29

Prayerfully read Romans 2:1-29.

Observe, Interpret, Apply
1. What main thought or scripture spoke to you from last week's lesson?

2. Prayerfully read Romans 2 in one sitting. In this chapter Paul is careful to show the guilt of both the moral man and the self-righteous Jew without Jesus Christ. What truth stands out to you as you read this chapter?

_____

_____

_____

_____

_____

3. Reread Romans 2. In the chart below write key words and phrases, and give a title to each passage.

Vs.	Romans 2:1-16	Vs.	Romans 2:17-29
Passage Title		**Passage Title**	

4. In Romans 2 Paul shows the hypocrisy of one sinner judging another. Look up Romans 14:4. How does this verse change the way you view fellow servants of God?

5. Read Matthew 7:1–5, and write it out in your own words.

6. Have you ever judged or felt judged by a fellow believer? If so, what was the resulting fruit?

7. Matthew 7:1–5 speaks about judging brothers and sisters in the church. The battle raging around us in this world is enough for believers to deal with; Christians don't need judgment from each other as well. We are to edify one another, building up instead of tearing down with a judgmental attitude. List some ways we could edify a brother or sister in Christ.

Day 2: Romans 2:1–11

Prayerfully read Romans 2:1–11.

Observe, Interpret, Apply

1. Reread Romans 2:1–6. To what is Paul referring as he begins this passage with the word "therefore"?

2. Genuine salvation comes from Jesus Christ and produces the righteousness of God in our lives. How does Galatians 5:16–18 instruct believers to walk?

3. What is produced if we do not "retain God in our knowledge," according to Galatians 5:19–21? Note the similarities between this passage and Romans 1:18–32.

4. What is the fruit of the Spirit? What attributes will be displayed in our lives as we walk in the Spirit? (See Gal. 5:22-25.)

5. According to Ephesians 5:5-12, how are believers to walk?

6. What is Paul's conclusion about what all believers were before salvation and what we will be and do after salvation, as seen in Ephesians 5:8-11?

7. What is your understanding of Paul's conclusion in the question above?

8. Often when we judge the behavior of others, we are doing the very same behaviors ourselves. According to Romans 2:5, what are the results of judging our brothers or sisters in a harsh manner, especially if we are guilty of doing the same things they are?

9. How will God render judgment to people, according to Romans 2:6?

10. Contrast the two groups of people listed in Romans 2:7–10.

11. When a person sins, it always affects others. When you are affected by someone else's sin, what are your immediate thoughts toward that person?

12. What is sin, according to 1 John 3:4?

13. Whom does David say sin is against in Psalm 51:4?

_____

_____

_____

_____

14. What do Romans 2:11 and Colossians 3:25 reveal? Write it below in your own words.

_____

_____

_____

_____

_____

> You, O Lord, are a God full of compassion, and gracious, longsuffering and abundant in mercy and truth.
>
> PSALM 86:15

15. When we realize that all sin is against God, the impartial Judge—the One before whom we will all stand to give account one day—how should we respond when a person's sin affects us?

_____

_____

_____

_____

_____

_____

16. What does the Lord of hosts say in Zechariah 7:9 regarding true justice?

_____

_____

_____

_____

_____

Day 3: Romans 2:12–14

Prayerfully read Romans 2:12–14.

Observe, Interpret, Apply

1. Why was the law given, according to the following verses?

    Galatians 3:24:

    Romans 7:7:

2. Look up Deuteronomy 11:27–28, and record what it says about obedience.

3. Who will be judged by the law, according to Romans 2:12?

4. Where does Hebrews 8:10 say God will write the law?

5. Write out Psalm 119:11 below.

6. God gave the law to the Jews, but how does Romans 8:3-4 say the law applies to Christians today?

7. According to 2 Corinthians 9:8, what enables us to live in a way that is pleasing to God?

8. Comment on the distinction Paul makes between the hearers and doers of the law in Romans 2:13.

9. How does James 1:22-25 confirm Romans 2:13-14?

> I will give them a heart to know Me, that I am the LORD; and they shall be My people, and I will be their God, for they shall return to Me with their whole heart.
>
> JEREMIAH 24:7

10. Why is it essential for us to respond to the Word of God when we hear it? (See Matt. 7:24–27.) Contrast the hearer only with the doer of the Word.

_____

_____

_____

_____

_____

_____

Day 4: Romans 2:14–20

Prayerfully read Romans 2:14–20.

Observe, Interpret, Apply

1. Read Romans 2:14–15 in several translations. Although Gentiles do not have God's written law, how do they show that they know it?

_____

_____

_____

2. What does this confirm from Romans 1:18–21?

_____

_____

_____

3. What bears witness to the law of God being written on people's hearts, according to Romans 2:15?

_____

_____

_____

4. Using your study tools, define "conscience" (Strong's #4893).

5. When your lifestyle is contrary to God's Word or His character, does your conscience *excuse* you or *accuse* you? Depending on how you answer, either thank God or ask Him to help you.

6. If you have been living in a way that you know is not bringing glory to God, ask the Holy Spirit not only to convict you but also to give you the power to stop. Record below what Hebrews 10:22–23 says can happen when we choose to seek forgiveness. Let it be your prayer today.

7. According to Romans 2:16, what will God judge?

8. Write out Hebrews 4:13.

9. Read Romans 2:17–20 and list ten things in which the Jews prided themselves.

1.
2.
3.
4.
5.
6.
7.
8.
9.
10.

10. Can any of the things listed above gain a person entrance into eternity? Why or why not?

> Not that we are sufficient of ourselves to think of anything as being from ourselves, but our sufficiency is from God.
>
> 2 CORINTHIANS 3:5

11. What perspective on worldly wisdom does Paul give in 1 Corinthians 3:18–19?

12. Record what James 4:6 says about pride.

13. Does this change your perspective regarding the things in which you pride yourself? Explain.

_____

_____

_____

_____

Day 5: Romans 2:21–29

Prayerfully read Romans 2:21-29.

Observe, Interpret, Apply
1. Sometimes we as Christians get caught up in hypocritical living, placing standards on others that are much higher than those we can maintain ourselves. Complete the following chart, listing the five problems the Jews had as seen in Romans 2:21-23.

High Standard Placed on Others	Actual Standard Placed on Themselves
1.	1.
2.	2.
3.	3.
4.	4.
5.	5.

2. How can you avoid hypocrisy in your life?

_____

_____

_____

THE POWER OF THE GOSPEL

3. How does 1 Corinthians 4:7 speak to your heart about avoiding hypocrisy?

_____

_____

_____

> Search me, O God,
> and know my heart;
> try me, and know
> my anxieties; and see
> if there is any wicked
> way in me, and lead me
> in the way everlasting.
>
> PSALM 139:23–24

4. The Jews valued rituals; these traditions made them feel that they could obtain favor with God. One of the most important rituals was circumcision. According to Genesis 17:9–14, why did the practice of circumcision begin?

_____

_____

_____

_____

5. What is more important to God—physical circumcision or spiritual circumcision? Look up the following scriptures to help you answer.

Galatians 6:15:

_____

_____

_____

Deuteronomy 30:6:

_____

_____

_____

1 Corinthians 7:18–19:

_____

_____

_____

6. Carefully read Hebrews 9:9–14, and record what it says about the rituals of the Jews in contrast to the work of Jesus.

7. Who is the only One who can fulfill the ordinances of the law set forth by God, according to the words of Jesus in Matthew 5:17?

8. Based on Romans 2:28–29, what is Paul's final conclusion regarding the ritual of circumcision?

9. The following quote by Warren Wiersbe is a summary of Paul's argument regarding Romans 2:27: "An obedient Gentile with no circumcision would be more acceptable than a disobedient Jew with circumcision. In fact, a disobedient Jew turns his circumcision into uncircumcision in God's sight, for God looks on the heart."[1] What does this tell you about the emphasis society places on outward appearances?

10. How does Paul describe a Jew in Romans 2:28–29?

11. What characterizes a change of heart?

> Judge nothing before the time, until the Lord comes, who will both bring to light the hidden things of darkness and reveal the counsels of the hearts. Then each one's praise will come from God.
>
> 1 CORINTHIANS 4:5

12. Have you been overly concerned about how you look to others? Is there something that you have been depending on for your salvation or spiritual growth other than the finished work of Christ? We have seen in our study this week that there is no ritual or act that we can do apart from trusting in His grace. It is not by our efforts or talents that we will please our Lord. Record Philippians 2:13 below, and allow God to speak to your heart about His provision for grace in your life.

13. Write a response to the Lord for all He has done, all He is doing, and all He will continue to do in and through your life for His glory.

Romans 3:1–31

Teach us, O God, that nothing is necessary to Thee.
Were anything necessary to Thee, that thing would be the measure of
Thine imperfection: and how could we worship one who is imperfect? If nothing is
necessary to Thee, then no one is necessary, and if no one, then not we. Thou dost
seek us though Thou does not need us. We seek Thee because we need Thee, for in
Thee we live and move and have our being. Amen.

A. W. TOZER

Day 1: Overview of Romans 3:1–31

Prayerfully read Romans 3:1–31.

Observe, Interpret, Apply

1. In Romans 1 Paul proved that man deserves the righteous wrath of God. In Romans 2 he addressed the self-righteousness of the one who trusts in his religion, pointing out that all the rituals under the sun will not make him righteous. Now in Romans 3 Paul first gives the bad news: "there is none righteous, no, not one" (Rom. 3:12); and then he gives the good news: the gospel is for Jews and Gentiles alike (see Rom. 3:29). Why do you think it was so hard for the Jews to accept this?

_____

_____

_____

_____

> He is a Jew who is one inwardly; and circumcision is that of the heart, in the Spirit, not in the letter; whose praise is not from men but from God.
>
> ROMANS 2:29

2. The religious people in Paul's day were wholly focused on the rituals of the outward man. What are some of the things we focus on today regarding outward behavior that give a righteous appearance?

3. While man looks at the outward appearance and judges according to what he can see, what does God look at, according to 1 Samuel 16:7?

> My conscience is clear, but that does not make me innocent. It is the Lord who judges me. Therefore judge nothing before the appointed time; wait till the Lord comes. He will bring to light what is hidden in darkness and will expose the motives of the heart. At that time each will receive their praise from God.
>
> 1 CORINTHIANS 4:4-5, NIV

4. Read Jeremiah 17:9-10. According to this verse, what is the condition of our hearts?

5. Since our hearts are wicked, how can we have hope in God's sight? Look up the following scriptures to help you answer.

Psalm 119:147:

Lamentations 3:24:

_____

_____

_____

6. Read Hebrews 10:19–24, and share how it ministers to you today.

_____

_____

_____

_____

_____

7. Prayerfully read through Romans 3. Using the chart below, record key words and phrases highlighting God's deliverance from condemnation. Then title each passage.

I will hope continually, and will praise You yet more and more. My mouth shall tell of Your righteousness and Your salvation all the day, for I do not know their limits. I will go in the strength of the Lord GOD; I will make mention of Your righteousness, of Yours only.

PSALM 71:14–16

Vs.	Romans 3:1-8	Vs.	Romans 3:9-20	Vs.	Romans 3:21-31

Passage Title	Passage Title	Passage Title

Day 2: Romans 3:1–8

Prayerfully read Romans 3:1–8.

Observe, Interpret, Apply
1. Paul knew that the Jews would have many questions about his teachings, because those teachings undid much that the Jews understood about their traditions regarding the Word of God. Anticipating their questions, Paul asked a series of questions and then answered them. In the chart below, record these questions and answers from Romans 3:1–8.

Anticipated Question	Answer
3:1:	3:2:
3:3:	3:4:
3:5:	3:6:

3:7:	No answer here
3:8:	3:8:

2. What were the advantages of the Jews being chosen of God, according to Romans 3:2?

3. What were the disadvantages of the Jews being chosen of God? Read the second half of Luke 12:48 to help you answer.

4. What were the Gentiles who believed in the finished work of Jesus Christ given upon repentance? See Acts 2:38–39 for your answer.

5. According to Romans 3:3–4 and 2 Timothy 2:11–13, does our unbelief void God's promises?

6. How would you respond to someone who said, "I can sin, because God's grace will cover it"?

7. Read Romans 3:5–8 below from the Living Bible:

> Some say, "Our breaking faith with God is good, our sins serve a good purpose, for people will notice how good God is when they see how bad we are. Is it fair, then, for him to punish us when our sins are helping him?" (That is the way some people talk.) God forbid! Then what kind of God would he be, to overlook sin? How could he ever condemn anyone? For he could not judge and condemn me as a sinner if my dishonesty brought him glory by pointing up his honesty in contrast to my lies. If you follow through with that idea you come to this: the worse we are, the better God likes it! But the damnation of those who say such things is just. Yet some claim that this is what I preach! (Rom. 3:5–8)

8. How does Romans 6:1–7 confirm the idea that the freedom we have in Christ is not freedom to sin but freedom *from* sin?

9. How are you to live your life in this world, according to 1 Peter 2:16–17?

10. In the King James Version, Romans 3:5 reads, "If our unrighteousness commend the righteousness of God, what shall we say? Is God unrighteous who taketh vengeance?" Using your study tools, define "vengeance" (Strong's #3709), and write its meaning below.

11. Do you think God is unjust if He takes vengeance upon (punishes) the wicked?

12. What is your role regarding vengeance, according to Romans 12:17–21?

13. Psalm 94:1 says vengeance belongs to whom?

Day 3: Romans 3:9–20

Prayerfully read Romans 3:9–20.

Observe, Interpret, Apply

1. In the chart below, key words from Romans 3:9–18 are listed. Read through the passage, observing what it says about these key words. List your findings in the appropriate columns.

Vs.	"They," "Their," "Whose"	Vs.	"None"

2. The point of these first few chapters of Romans is not to cause hopelessness and despair over our sin but to give us hope and to challenge us to seek right relationship with God through the Lord Jesus Christ. We must *never* minimize our sin. The Bible is very clear: "There is none righteous, no, not one" (Rom. 3:10). We must never ignore or neglect the truth that the only way to God is through the shed blood of Jesus Christ. We will never recognize the need for His grace if we don't recognize the seriousness of our sin. But praise be to God for His grace that is greater than sin.

When Moses' father-in-law came to Moses with the advice that he appoint judges over the people, he recognized the need for people to view themselves seriously before God. What four traits did he instruct Moses to look for, according to Exodus 18:21–22?

3. What does it mean to fear God?

4. Using your study tools, look up the word "fear" from Romans 3:18, and write out its definition (Strong's #5401).

5. What should we fear, according to Hebrews 4:1–2?

6. Why should we fear God, according to the following verses?

Psalm 145:19–20:

Hebrews 5:7:

Hebrews 12:28–29:

7. How can we fear God with a reverential fear? Look up the following verses to help you answer.

Jeremiah 32:40:

Philippians 2:12–13:

8. Take time out right now and thank God for His sovereign work in your life, and ask Him to increase this work in you. List below some ways He has worked in your life in the past.

9. Read Romans 3:19–20. According to the following verses, what is the law?

Romans 3:20:

Galatians 3:24:

10. What is the directive for those who have "crucified the flesh with its passions and desires" (Gal. 5:24–26)?

11. Often the law and the grace of Jesus Christ seem contrary to each other. According to Matthew 5:17, how do the law and Jesus Christ relate?

12. How does this connection relate to the life of a believer, according to Romans 8:4?

Day 4: Romans 3:21–31

Prayerfully read Romans 3:21–31.

Observe, Interpret, Apply

1. Define "justify" using your study tools (Strong's #1344). Write out a definition using your own words.

_____

_____

_____

_____

_____

> Behold, I come;
> in the scroll of the book
> it is written of me.
> I delight to do Your will,
> O my God, and Your law
> is within my heart.
>
> PSALM 40:7-8

2. Look up Philippians 3:9. What is the key to partaking in God's righteousness?

_____

_____

_____

_____

> The righteousness of God
> is revealed from faith to
> faith; as it is written, "The
> just shall live by faith."
>
> ROMANS 1:17

3. Romans 3:22 says that the righteousness of God is for "all who believe." How do the following verses support this?

Colossians 3:11:

_____

_____

_____

Acts 15:8-9:

4. What does Ecclesiastes 7:20 mean: "There is not a just man on earth who does good and does not sin"? See Romans 3:23 to help you answer.

5. How are we justified, according to the following scriptures?

Romans 3:24:

Know that only those who are of faith are sons of Abraham. And the Scripture, foreseeing that God would justify the Gentiles by faith, preached the gospel to Abraham beforehand, saying, "In you all the nations shall be blessed." So then those who are of faith are blessed with believing Abraham.

GALATIANS 3:7-9

Romans 5:9:

1 Corinthians 6:11:

Galatians 2:16:

Titus 3:7:

6. What is the common thread in all the above verses?

7. Why did Jesus have to die for our sin, according to 1 Peter 1:18–20? Use other translations to amplify your answer.

8. Using your study tools, define "propitiation" (Strong's #2435) in the context of Romans 3:25.

9. Define "propitiation" in your own words.

_____

_____

_____

_____

Day 5: Romans 3:27–31

Prayerfully read Romans 3:27-31.

Observe, Interpret, Apply

1. As you realize what Jesus has done in becoming the propitiation for your sins, explain why you think Paul words Romans 3:27 the way he does.

_____

_____

_____

_____

_____

The righteousness of God apart from the law is revealed, . . . even the righteousness of God, through faith in Jesus Christ, to all and on all who believe. . . . For all have sinned and fall short of the glory of God, being justified freely by His grace through the redemption that is in Christ Jesus.

ROMANS 3:21-24

2. What does Paul conclude, according to Romans 3:28?

_____

_____

_____

3. The word "justification" means "to render (i.e., show or regard as) just or innocent."[1] Some say it means "just as if you have never sinned a day in your life." Stop and think about what Jesus has done for you personally. What response should this cause in your life?

_____

_____

_____

4. In Romans 3:29, Paul asks two rhetorical questions. How does Paul answer those questions in Romans 3:29–30?

> Your Maker is your husband, the LORD of hosts is His name; and your Redeemer is the Holy One of Israel; He is called the God of the whole earth.
>
> ISAIAH 54:5

5. Since God is the "God of the whole earth" (Isa. 54:5) and Jesus is the propitiation for our sins, what should our heart's desire be toward the lost, according to the following verses?

Matthew 28:19:

Mark 16:15:

1 Peter 3:15:

6. Define "establish" (Strong's #2476) from Romans 3:31.

7. Some have argued that Paul seems to make void the law because of his emphasis on faith in Christ. Knowing this, Paul declares in Romans 3:31, "If we emphasize faith, does this mean that we can forget about the law? Of course not! In fact, only when we have faith do we truly fulfill the law" (NLT). Compare this with Galatians 5:14, and share how faith in Christ enables us to fulfill, establish, or stand in the law.

8. Because of God's love for you, because He sent Jesus as the propitiation for your sins, because you are justified by faith in the finished work on the cross, because you are forgiven and free to now come boldly before the throne of grace to find help in time of need, and because you have access to God Almighty, what does the Lord require of you, according to Micah 6:8?

> Salvation is the work of God in the heart, made possible by the work of God on the Cross. No man can forgive his own sins, no man can declare himself justified and clean. All this is the work of God in a man.
>
> A. W. TOZER

Digging Deeper (Optional)
While it is optional to look up the following verses that show the triune nature of God, please look up at least two, as this topic is one all believers should be acquainted with.

Who is this "one God" Paul writes of in Romans 3:30? Look up the following verses to help you answer. These verses will also help you when witnessing to the lost, those who deny the deity of Jesus Christ.

John 1:1:

John 1:14:

John 10:30–33:

John 17:5:

John 20:27–29:

Hebrews 1:3–4:

Colossians 1:15–20:

Romans 4:1–25

*The promise that he would be the heir of the world was not to Abraham
or to his seed through the law, but through the righteousness of faith.*

ROMANS 4:13

Day 1: Overview of Romans 4:1–25

Prayerfully read Romans 4:1–25. Remember to read with a purpose as you
begin this new section. Allow it to be fresh each time you read it, asking
yourself who, what, where, when, why and how.

Our study of Romans thus far has shown that all are condemned in sin
and have a great need for God's righteousness. The Gentiles are guilty; the
Jews are guilty; *all* are guilty before God! Our guilt only shows our need for
God's righteousness; it contrasts His righteousness with condemnation. It
has been established that our lives as Christians exist only by God's grace.
The life of Christ living in and through us—that is the hope of glory!

Observe, Interpret, Apply
1. Romans 4 offers an illustration of the truth proclaimed in Romans 3.
What is one truth that stood out for you from last week's lesson?

....

_____

2. From your reading of Romans 4, write key words and phrases in the chart below, and give each passage a title. Note how Paul says that we are justified (declared righteous).

Vs.	Romans 4:1–8	Vs.	Romans 4:9–17	Vs.	Romans 4:18–25

Passage Title		Passage Title		Passage Title	

3. Whom does Paul use to illustrate righteousness?

4. How do we as Christians uphold the law?

> He did not waver at the promise of God through unbelief, but was strengthened in faith, giving glory to God.
>
> ROMANS 4:20

5. Look up the following verses, and comment on each one.

   Hebrews 10:14–18:

   Galatians 2:19–21:

6. Do you have complete faith in Jesus—not only for salvation but also for righteous living? Write a prayer asking God to strengthen your faith as you are reminded of who He is!

Whatever God felt about anything, He still feels. Whatever He thought about anyone, He still thinks. Whatever He approved, He still approves. Whatever He condemned, He still condemns. Today we have what they call the relativity of morals. But remember this: God never changes. Holiness and righteousness are conformity to the will of God. And the will of God never changes for moral creatures.

A. W. TOZER

Digging Deeper (Optional)

Read the following two events that record times when Abraham believed God. How do you think you would react if you were in his situation?

Genesis 15:1–6:

Genesis 22:1–18:

Day 2: David in Light of Romans 4

Read a portion of David's life from 2 Samuel 11:2–12:13.

Observe, Interpret, Apply

1. What was David's sin in 2 Samuel 11:2–4?

2. What did David say to Nathan in 2 Samuel 12:13 that indicates repentance?

3. David was not a perfect man; he sinned like all people do (see Rom. 3:23). But he repented of his sin. If righteousness were according to our works, David would never have been able to claim righteousness. But Paul says in Romans 4:6-8, "David also describes the blessedness of the man to whom God imputes righteousness apart from works: 'Blessed are those whose lawless deeds are forgiven,

> If we confess our sins, He is faithful and just to forgive us our sins and to cleanse us from all unrighteousness.
>
> 1 JOHN 1:9

and whose sins are covered; blessed is the man to whom the LORD shall not impute sin.'" Record below how Psalm 32:1-2 supports what Paul says in Romans 4:6-8.

4. Before time began God knew David would sin; nevertheless, how was David described in Acts 13:22?

Day 3: Romans 4:1-8

Prayerfully read Romans 4:1-8.

Observe, Interpret, Apply

1. The Jews gloried in Abraham, considering him one of the greatest saints ever to live. It must have been a great shock to the Jews for Paul to say that Abraham had nothing to offer God in the flesh but was justified by simple faith, as any common sinner is. It was God who made the promise, and it

was God who fulfilled the promise; the only thing Abraham did was take God at His word. Abraham did nothing other than simply believe, and his faith was accounted to him as righteousness! Considering all this, whom do you consider great today?

2. Who alone works righteousness in every believer?

3. According to Isaiah 42:8, who alone is to get all glory?

4. What did Abraham have to boast about, according to Romans 4:2–3?

5. What in our flesh is there to boast about?

6. Paul called Abraham his father. He was reminding his readers that he himself was a Jew. If you study the life of Paul, you will see that he has more to boast about than just about anyone. Look up Philippians 3:3–6, and comment on how Paul describes himself in the flesh.

7. Paul knew what it was like to live in the perfection of his pedigree and religious standing without the Spirit of God in his life. What does he conclude in Philippians 3:7–11?

8. The ultimate downfall of Adam and Eve was their desire for greater knowledge (see Gen. 3:1-6). The Jews thought their righteousness came from what they knew about God, as some do today. Be sure you are not basing your righteousness on what you know about doctrine or about God but rather on your faith in Jesus and His ability to make you righteous. As you search the Scriptures, pray for the desire to seek a more intimate relationship with Jesus. In this regard, for what did Jesus rebuke the Pharisees in John 5:39-40?

9. What should be our goal, according to Ephesians 3:19?

10. Whose help are we to seek when searching the Scriptures? (See John 14:26.)

11. In Romans 4:4–5 we see the principle of man working and receiving wages that are due. We understand this principle in our own lives practically, but how does this principle translate spiritually to our relationship with God?

Behold! The Lamb of God who takes away the sin of the world!

JOHN 1:29

12. According to Romans 4:4, if we were to work at our salvation (and sanctification), what is it that we would receive? What would it not be?

13. Whom does God justify, according to Romans 4:5?

14. Is there anyone whom God cannot declare justified?

15. According to Romans 4:6, what one word describes the man or woman who has faith that is accounted as righteousness?

16. Note in Romans 4:8 that Paul is quoting David. Acknowledging the fact that David sinned in the sight of God, Paul quotes from Psalm 32:2: "Blessed is the man to whom the LORD does not impute iniquity." Does this mean David did not pay consequences for his sin? (See 2 Sam. 12:15-18.)

17. What does Galatians 6:7-8 say about consequences?

18. Does being forgiven mean we will never pay consequences? Explain your answer.

19. If David could pronounce, "Blessed is he . . . whose sin is covered" (Ps. 32:1), how much more should we rejoice, knowing that Christ has come to remove our sin once and for all! Look up Hebrews 9:24-28 to fully understand this principle; then write a thank-you note to Jesus.

Digging Deeper (Optional)
Read Leviticus 16, and describe the scapegoat from Leviticus 16:10.

How does this point to Jesus Christ?

Day 4: Romans 4:9–17

Because Jesus Christ died, because He was God and because He was man, His atonement was absolutely and fully efficacious. All the attributes of God are on the side of the person who confesses his or her sin and turns and runs to the feet of Jesus.

A. W. TOZER

Prayerfully read Romans 4:9–17.

Observe, Interpret, Apply
1. Look up the word "blessedness" (Strong's #3108) using your study tools, and write out its definition.

2. According to Romans 4:9, upon whom does "this blessedness" come?

3. It is important to note that God counted Abraham righteous fourteen or fifteen years before circumcision was implemented. To Abraham and the world, circumcision was an outward sign, much like baptism is to Christians today. Romans 4:11 says that Abraham "received the sign of circumcision, a seal of the righteousness of the faith which he had while still uncircumcised." Using your study tools, do a word study on "sealed" (Strong's #4973). As you answer the following questions, think about the meaning of this precious promise! First, how and when are believers today sealed, according to Ephesians 1:13–14?

How:

When:

4. Second, for what are we sealed, according to Ephesians 4:30?

5. Finally, read Colossians 2:10–15, and write out a response below.

6. What does Romans 4:16 say that our faith is "according to"? What does this assure the believer in Jesus?

7. According to the following verses, from where does our faith come?

Romans 12:3:

Romans 10:17:

8. Read Hebrews 6:11–12. What does the writer of Hebrews say is his desire?

9. What does the Hebrews passage above say will happen to those who are diligent to seek God?

10. Read Joshua 4:5-7. Why did the Lord tell Joshua to take stones from the Jordan?

_____

_____

_____

_____

11. Do you have "stones of remembrance"? Take a moment and ask the Lord to show you the stones of remembrance (times when God has shown Himself faithful in your life) you can pass down as a memorial to your children or the next generation. Write a brief version of them here.

_____

_____

_____

_____

_____

_____

_____

Day 5: Romans 4:16–25

Prayerfully read Romans 4:16-25.

Observe, Interpret, Apply
1. As way of review, define the following words.

"Faith" from Romans 4:16 (Strong's #4102):

_____

_____

_____

"Hope" from Romans 4:18 (Strong's #1680):

_____

_____

_____

> Faith makes the ways of God pleasant and admirable, but unbelief makes them heavy and hard. Faith will comfort in the midst of fears, but unbelief causeth fears in the midst of comforts. Faith bringeth us near to God when we are far from Him, but unbelief puts us far from God when we are near to Him.
>
> JOHN BUNYAN

2. Romans 4:19 notes the physical conditions of Abraham and Sarah at the time of the fulfillment of God's promise to them. This clearly shows the great faith Abraham had, since the promise was a physical impossibility. Why do you think God waited so long to fulfill His promise to Abraham?

_____

_____

_____

_____

_____

_____

_____

3. Have you given up on God? Has your faith wavered because of having to wait for Him for a long time? Record how 2 Peter 3:8–9 helps you in your situation today.

_____

_____

_____

_____

4. God often waits with us like He did with Abraham. How does Isaiah 55:8–9 encourage you when your situation seems to be on hold?

_____

_____

_____

_____

_____

_____

_____

_____

_____

_____

_____

I wait for the LORD,
my soul waits, and in His
word I do hope. My soul
waits for the LORD more
than those who watch for
the morning—yes, more
than those who watch
for the morning.

PSALM 130:5-6

5. From Romans 4:19–21, write out the four key phases of Abraham's faith that accounted him righteous before God. Underline the one that speaks to you today.

Romans 4:19	Romans 4:20a	Romans 4:20b	Romans 4:21

6. Why was Romans 4:19–21 recorded in Scripture, according to verses 23–24?

_____

_____

_____

7. What does Isaiah 53:5 say about the crucifixion of Jesus Christ?

> There comes a time when a man ceases from his own works, hearing that Christ finished the work, paid the ransom, at the cross. Then he rests! Such a soul, knowing himself to be a sinner and ungodly, believes on God, just as he is, and knows he is welcome.
>
> WILLIAM NEWELL

_____

_____

_____

_____

8. Why is the resurrection of Jesus Christ so important, according to the following verses?

Romans 4:25:

_____

_____

_____

Romans 8:34:

_____

_____

_____

1 Corinthians 15:17:

_____

_____

_____

_____

9. Look up Philippians 3:10–11. Meditate on what this means, and allow it to be your heart's desire today!

> This is eternal life, that they may know You, the only true God, and Jesus Christ whom You have sent.
>
> JOHN 17:3

Digging Deeper (Optional)
By way of review this week, we see that Paul continues to elaborate on the superiority of faith over the works of the law. Complete the statements below as you keep in mind what you have been studying in Romans 1-4.

Faith came before what two things?

_____

_____

Faith does what the law cannot; what is the law incapable of accomplishing?

_____

_____

_____

Faith assures believers of salvation because it is based on what?

_____

_____

_____

Faith glorifies God by highlighting what?

_____

_____

> He did not waver at the promise of God through unbelief, but was strengthened in faith, giving glory to God, and being fully convinced that what He had promised He was also able to perform.
>
> ROMANS 4:20-21

What quality of God does man's faith showcase?

_____

_____

_____

To whom is faith available?

_____

_____

_____

Ask God to strengthen your faith today!

Romans 5:1–21

Our Father, we know that Thou art present with us, but our knowledge
is but a figure and shadow of truth and has little of the spiritual savor and inward
sweetness such knowledge should afford. This is for us a great loss and the cause of
much weakness of heart. Help us to make at once such amendment of life
as is necessary before we can experience the true meaning of the words
"In Thy presence is fullness of joy." Amen.

A. W. TOZER

Day 1: Overview of Romans 5:1–21

Prayerfully read Romans 5:1–21.

God's grace is powerful. It is able to declare us righteous, reconcile us to God, grant us access to God, certify our hope, and even bring purpose to all our earthly afflictions. Sin has reigned since Adam, and all men have sinned, but the power of grace is far greater than the power of sin.

But although God's grace has the power to forgive and set men free from sin, it is not a blanket we throw over our sin to cover it up. God's grace is His divine influence on our hearts that is meant to keep us from sinning in the first place. Whereas sin brought death, God's grace brings life! It is in this amazing manifold grace of God that believers stand before a righteous God.

In Romans 5 Paul declares the benefits and superiority of God's grace and explains how this grace is made available to us through faith. As you read the passages this week, look for and note your observations about God's grace.

This week we will be looking up many scriptures, so if you feel overwhelmed, when you come to the questions with multiple verses, choose only two verses to look up. As you read and write out the scriptures, allow the Spirit of God to impress each one upon your heart. Spend some time in prayer thanking Him for what He will show you in your study this week.

Observe, Interpret, Apply

1. Read 2 Timothy 3:16–17. Since God inspires all Scripture, why do you suppose He devoted so much of the book of Romans to revealing the wretchedness of man?

2. Read through Romans 5 again and, using the chart below, pull out key words and phrases. Then title each passage.

Vs.	Romans 5:1–5	Vs.	Romans 5:6–11	Vs.	Romans 5:12–21

Passage Title	Passage Title	Passage Title

3. Romans 5 begins with the word "therefore," which always shows that Paul is about to speak of a *result* from previous verses. What is Romans 5:1 a result of?

4. What are some of the results of God's grace in our lives, according to Romans 5:1–2?

5. Look up the following verses, and comment on where we are to place our hope.

Psalm 119:81:

Ephesians 1:18–19:

Colossians 1:27:

Titus 1:2:

Titus 2:13:

6. If God is a loving God, why does He allow His children to suffer tribulations? Back up your answer with Scripture.

7. How does "knowing that tribulation produces perseverance; and perseverance, character; and character, hope" (Rom. 5:3) affect your perspective concerning tribulations in your life?

8. Share a way in which God has brought purpose through tribulation in your life.

9. When difficult circumstances arise, it is easy to become discouraged, ashamed, or disappointed. What does Romans 5:5 say about hope?

> Having been justified by faith, we have peace with God through our Lord Jesus Christ, through whom also we have access by faith into this grace in which we stand, and rejoice in hope of the glory of God.
>
> ROMANS 5:1-2

10. Oh, that God would give us His perspective of joy when various trials come our way! Write out James 1:2-4, and pray that God would truly work this perspective in your heart.

Digging Deeper (Optional)
Using your study tools, define the words below from Romans 5:3-4: "We also glory in tribulations, knowing that tribulation produces perseverance; and perseverance, character; and character, hope."

"Tribulations" (Strong's #2347):

"Perseverance," or "patience" (Strong's #5281):

"Character" ("experience" in KJV) (Strong's #1382):

"Hope" (Strong's #1680):

Day 2: Romans 5:5–11

Prayerfully read Romans 5:5-11.

Observe, Interpret, Apply

1. Read Titus 3:4–8. What appeared toward man? How?

2. According to Titus 3:7, how are you justified, and what does that ensure?

_____

_____

_____

_____

3. For God to pour out into you, you must be willing to be poured into. How does the Word of God describe you as a believer in Jesus Christ? (See 2 Tim. 2:20–21.)

_____

_____

_____

_____

> The highest glory of the creature is in being a vessel, to receive and enjoy and show forth the glory of God. It can do this only as it is willing to be nothing in itself, that God may be everything.
>
> ANDREW MURRAY

4. Look up the following verses that confirm Romans 5:5. What do we contain, or manifest, if we belong to Christ?

1 Corinthians 3:16 (speaking of the church):

_____

_____

1 Corinthians 6:19–20 (speaking of an individual believer):

_____

_____

Philippians 1:20:

_____

_____

_____

John 14:17:

John 7:37–39:

> If we cooperate with Him in loving obedience, God will manifest Himself to us, and that manifestation will be the difference between a nominal Christian life and a life radiant with the light of His face.
>
> A. W. TOZER

5. For whom do Romans 5:6 and 5:8 say that Christ died?

6. The love God has for His creation far exceeds any love we can comprehend. The only way we can love God or one another is by receiving the agape love He places in our hearts. Jesus is our ultimate example of how we are to love one another. Look up the following verses and record the example Jesus set for us.

John 15:13–14:

Galatians 2:20:

7. Using your study tools, define the word "wrath" (Strong's #3709) used in Romans 5:9, and write its meaning below.

8. Many think that if God is a God of love, He cannot be a God of wrath. Record John 3:16–19.

> A new commandment I give to you, that you love one another; as I have loved you, that you also love one another. By this all will know that you are My disciples, if you have love for one another.
>
> JOHN 13:34–35

9. Explain in your own words how these two characteristics of God—love and wrath—coexist.

10. According to the following verses, what provision did our loving God give to each of us in place of the wrath we deserve?

1 John 2:2:

Hebrews 2:17–18:

> When God justifies a
> sinner, everything in God
> is on the sinner's side.
>
> A. W. TOZER

11. Look up Deuteronomy 32:3–4, and list the characteristics of God. Write a prayer of praise for who He is and what He has done for you.

Day 3: Romans 5:10–14

Prayerfully read Romans 5:10–14.

Observe, Interpret, Apply

1. *Nelson's Illustrated Bible Dictionary* gives the following statement about crucifixion:

> Crucifixion was the method of torture and execution used by the Romans to put Christ to death. At a crucifixion the victim usually was nailed or tied to a wooden stake and left to die.
>
> Crucifixion was used by many nations of the ancient world, including Assyria, Media, and Persia. . . . The Romans later adopted this method and used it often throughout their empire. This was the Romans' most severe form of execution; so it was reserved only for slaves and criminals. No Roman citizen could be crucified. . . .
>
> To the Jewish people, crucifixion represented the most disgusting form of death: "He who is hanged is accursed of God" (Deuteronomy 21:23; Galatians 3:13).[1]

Although crucifixion was a horrible type of death, as well as unlawful, especially according to Jewish law, what does Scripture say was Jesus' response to His own death on the cross?

Isaiah 53:7:

1 Peter 2:21–23:

Philippians 2:7–8:

2. In light of Jesus' example, how should we respond when others come against us?

3. Even though the religious leaders were smug as they watched Jesus being put to death, who was ultimately in control, according to John 10:17–18?

4. What important truth from Proverbs 21:1 should you remember when things seem to be spinning out of control?

5. It has been said that we cannot experience Pentecost, or the full blessing of the Holy Spirit, without the crucifixion. List the benefits of the crucifixion from the verses in the chart below:

Ephesians 2:13–19	Hebrews 9:22–28

6. Note that in Romans 5, Paul reiterates an idea already established throughout the book of Romans.

Romans 5:9: How are we saved through Jesus' death?

_____

_____

_____

Romans 5:10: How are we saved through His resurrection?

_____

_____

_____

7. In Galatians 2:20, Paul says, "I have been crucified with Christ; it is no longer I who live, but Christ lives in me; and the life which I now live in the flesh I live by faith in the Son of God, who loved me and gave Himself for me." What does it mean to be crucified with Christ? (See Col. 3:3–4.)

_____

_____

_____

_____

Totally apart from Law, and purely by Grace, we have a salvation that takes care of the past, the present, and the future. Christ died for us; Christ lives for us; Christ is coming for us! Hallelujah, what a Savior!

WARREN WIERSBE

8. Through our study thus far in Romans, we have established the fact that we were once alienated from God due to our sin. Read 1 Corinthians 6:9–11. Note that the key to this passage is the word "were." Take some time to thank God for the blood that He shed on your behalf! Write your thanksgiving below.

_____

_____

_____

_____

This is the testimony: that God has given us eternal life, and this life is in His Son. He who has the Son has life; he who does not have the Son of God does not have life. These things I have written to you who believe in the name of the Son of God, that you may know that you have eternal life, and that you may continue to believe in the name of the Son of God.

1 JOHN 5:11–13

9. Look up the word "reconciled" (Strong's #2644) using your study tools, and write out its definition.

Day 4: Romans 5:14–21

Prayerfully read Romans 5:14–21.

Observe, Interpret, Apply

1. Paul contrasts the original sin of Adam with the forgiveness of sin through Christ. In the columns below, record what the following scriptures say about each man.

First Adam	Second Adam
Genesis 2:7	Hebrews 4:15
1 Corinthians 15:22	1 Corinthians 15:22
1 Corinthians 15:45	1 Corinthians 15:45

1 Corinthians 15:46	1 Corinthians 15:46
1 Corinthians 15:47	1 Corinthians 15:47
1 Corinthians 15:48	1 Corinthians 15:48
Romans 5:12	Romans 5:15

2. We see stark contrasts between the result of Adam's life and that of Jesus' life. Read Romans 5:14–20, and considering the chart above, summarize the contrast in your own words.

Result of the first Adam's life:

Result of the second Adam's (Jesus') life:

3. According to Romans 5:21, what reigns in death? What reigns through righteousness?

4. Through whom alone does eternal life reign?

5. How would you answer someone who says that all roads lead to God?

6. Record what the following scriptures say about the way to eternal life with God.

Acts 4:12:

John 3:3:

Matthew 7:13–14:

7. After reading these scriptures, if you have not been born again, pray and ask God to come into your life right now! Read Romans 10:9–10 for further instruction.

8. Finish your time today by praying for an unsaved friend or relative. Try to commit some of the scriptures from today's study to memory so you will

know how to answer those who think there is a way to heaven other than through Jesus Christ.

> I am the way, the truth, and the life. No one comes to the Father except through Me.
>
> JOHN 14:6

Day 5: Review of Romans 5:1–21

Prayerfully read Romans 5:1–21.

Observe, Interpret, Apply

1. What does the phrase "having been justified" (Rom. 5:1) mean in your life? Write a response to the Lord for what He has done for you.

> You cannot help being in Adam, for this came by your first birth over which you had no control. But you can help staying in Adam, for you can experience a second birth—a new birth from above will put you in Christ. That is why Jesus said "Ye must be born again" in John 3:7.
>
> WARREN WIERSBE

2. According to Romans 5:1–2, what must happen before we can be at "peace with God"?

3. Through whom do "we have access . . . into this grace" (Rom. 5:2)?

4. How do we access this peace with God that Romans 5:1–2 speaks of?

_____

_____

_____

> We also glory in tribulations, knowing that tribulation produces perseverance; and perseverance, character; and character, hope. Now hope does not disappoint, because the love of God has been poured out in our hearts by the Holy Spirit who was given to us.
>
> ROMANS 5:3–5

5. How do we access grace to stand, according to Romans 5:2?

_____

_____

_____

6. In what do we rejoice?

_____

_____

7. According to the following verses, why are we to glory in tribulations?

2 Corinthians 1:3–4:

_____

_____

_____

1 Thessalonians 5:16–18:

_____

_____

_____

8. What does it mean to glory in tribulations?

_____

_____

_____

_____

_____

9. While you were still in your sin, God gave His only begotten Son as a sacrifice for your life. What does this say to you?

10. To close out this week's study, review what Romans 5 says about God's grace.

Romans 5:1–5: What is the *benefit* of God's grace?

Romans 5:6–7: What is the *work* of God's grace?

Romans 5:8–11: What is the *power* of God's grace?

Romans 5:12–14: What is our *need* for God's grace?

When we were
still without strength,
in due time Christ died
for the ungodly.

ROMANS 5:6

Romans 5:15–21: Comment on the *superiority* of God's grace.

_____

_____

_____

_____

_____

Romans 6:1–23

Oh to be nothing, nothing! Only to lie at His feet,
A broken and emptied vessel, for the master's use made meek.
Emptied, that He might fill me as forth to His service I go;
Broken, that so unhindered, His life through me might flow.

GEORGIANA M. TAYLOR

Day 1: Overview of Romans 6:1–23

Prayerfully read Romans 6:1–23.

Observe, Interpret, Apply

1. Begin in Romans 5:20, and read through Romans 6. Note key words or phrases, and list them in the chart below. Title each passage, and then title Romans 6. (Some of the key words in Romans 6 are "life," "death," "sin," "know," "consider," "present," and "obedient.")

Vs.	Romans 6:1-10	Vs.	Romans 6:11-12	Vs.	Romans 6:13-23

Passage Title	Passage Title	Passage Title
Chapter Title or Summary Statement		

2. Record what Romans 5:20–21 says as it leads into Romans 6.

_____

_____

_____

_____

_____

3. We often think of ministers as never having struggles with the flesh. What does the apostle Paul declare in 1 Timothy 1:12–16 about himself before he knew Christ?

_____

_____

4. In Romans 6:1 Paul states, "What shall we say then? Shall we continue in sin that grace may abound?" Some who stress the law use this verse to validate their position against grace teaching. No doubt Paul was asked this very question time and again by legalists who hounded and fought against him, not understanding the wonderful grace of God. The Pharisees criticized Paul's preaching of justification based solely on the free grace of God, arguing that if forgiveness is by grace, then is sin not a good thing? Should we not continue in sin so that God will have more of an opportunity to show His grace in our lives and become more magnified and glorified?

In Romans 6:2 Paul uses a phrase that contains the strongest Greek idiom for repudiating a statement. His response exudes a sense of outrage that anyone would ever think that it was fine to continue in sin. What is this response of Paul to the idea that one should sin so that the grace of God would abound?

5. What logical conclusion does Paul draw in Romans 6:2? How does Galatians 2:20 confirm this?

THE POWER OF THE GOSPEL

6. Does this mean that we will never sin again? Why or why not? Be sure to back your answer with Scripture.

Day 2: Romans 6:3–11

Prayerfully read Romans 6:3–11.

> It is beautiful to say, "I am crucified with Christ," and know that Christ is making your plans. I tell you, twenty minutes on your knees in silence before God will sometimes teach you more than you can learn out of books and teach you more than you can even learn in churches. And the Lord will give you your plans, and lay them before you.
>
> A. W. TOZER

Observe, Interpret, Apply

1. Read Romans 6:3–5, and record what it says about our lives.

2. Who has eternal life with God, according to the following scriptures?

John 1:12–13:

Galatians 3:26–27:

What is our "hope of glory," according to Colossians 1:27?

3. The believer's position in Christ shows the utter impossibility of a true believer continuing in sin. The word "continue" in this context means to practice or habitually yield to sin. A true believer no longer practices sin and no longer yields to sin as a lifestyle. It is true that we cannot live without *ever* sinning, yet if we are truly believers, we no longer live in sin. Read 1 John 1:6-10, and explain this in your own words.

4. Explain what you think it means to walk in newness of life.

5. What do we know, according to Romans 6:6?

6. The "old self" is referred to only three times in the New Testament. Look up the following references, noting the context of each one, and comment on what you learn regarding your old life before you came to Christ.

Romans 6:6–10:

May we be
John 3:16–17
people in a
Colossians 3:5–7
world!

Ephesians 4:20–24:

Colossians 3:5–11:

7. What does Galatians 5:1 say?

8. What is the liberty, or freedom, Galatians 5:1 speaks of?

9. Using your study tools, find out the definition of "bondage" in Galatians 5:1 (Strong's #1397), and write it below.

_____

_____

_____

_____

10. Read Romans 6:1-11, and note the contrast between death and life in the chart below.

Dead, Died, or Buried	Life, Live, or Alive

Day 3: Romans 6:12–13

Prayerfully read Romans 6:12-13.

Observe, Interpret, Apply

1. Read Romans 6:12-13. What does this scripture mean by "mortal body"?

2. How does sin manifest itself in our mortal bodies?

James 3:5-6:

> Choose for yourselves this day whom you will serve.
>
> JOSHUA 24:15

1 Corinthians 6:9-10:

3. Reread Romans 1:28-32. How does this relate to the verses above?

4. We can become proud when we do not see our own actions in the lists of sins throughout Scripture. When this happens, we can begin to point

fingers at others. How does 1 Corinthians 6:11 bring things into perspective for us?

_____

_____

_____

_____

_____

5. Look up the following words in the context of Romans 6:12–13.

"Present," or "yield" (Strong's #3936):

_____

_____

"Members" (Strong's #3196):

_____

_____

_____

"Instruments" (Strong's #3696):

_____

_____

A good tree does not bear bad fruit, nor does a bad tree bear good fruit. For every tree is known by its own fruit. For men do not gather figs from thorns, nor do they gather grapes from a bramble bush. A good man out of the good treasure of his heart brings forth good; and an evil man out of the evil treasure of his heart brings forth evil. For out of the abundance of the heart his mouth speaks.

LUKE 6:43-45

6. What does Paul "beseech" us to do in Romans 12:1–2? Write these verses out, and commit them to memory.

_____

_____

_____

_____

_____

_____

> It is done! I am the Alpha and the Omega, the Beginning and the End. I will give of the fountain of the water of life freely to him who thirsts. He who overcomes shall inherit all things, and I will be his God and he shall be My son.
>
> REVELATION 21:6–7

7. The life we live in Christ is only and all by the grace of God. However, we have an option, or a choice, to receive it. How can we fulfill our desire to have Christ living in and through us? Read Galatians 5:16 to help you answer.

_____

_____

_____

_____

_____

_____

Digging Deeper (Optional)
Look up Genesis 22:2–18 and Daniel 3:8–29, two passages that speak of people who presented their bodies as living sacrifices. Read these accounts, and comment on what you see as a common denominator between them. (Note: While Abraham offered up Isaac, some commentators say that Isaac was in his twenties, old enough to know what was happening and to resist, and therefore willingly offered himself up.)

_____

_____

_____

_____

_____

Day 4: Romans 6:14–23

Prayerfully read Romans 6:14–23, taking some time to pray before you read.

Observe, Interpret, Apply

1. Using your study tools, define the word "dominion" in Romans 6:14 (Strong's #2961).

2. Why does sin no longer have dominion over a Christian?

> Do not let sin control your puny body any longer; do not give in to its sinful desires. Do not let any part of your bodies become tools of wickedness, to be used for sinning; but give yourselves completely to God—every part of you—for you are back from death and you want to be tools in the hands of God, to be used for his good purposes.
>
> ROMANS 6:12–13, TLB

3. The word "slave" comes from the Greek root word *deho*. This root word means to be bound or tied—the opposite of freedom. In Romans 6:16 the Bible says we have a choice as to whom we will be slaves. What does it mean to "obey" sin?

4. What will happen if we yield to the lust of our flesh?

5. Read Matthew 6:24, and ask God to purge from you anything that is hindering your undivided service to Him.

6. We are often tempted to sin, but we don't actually sin unless we give in to the temptation. What example did Jesus leave for us in Hebrews 4:15?

7. What provision does God give us in our temptations, according to Hebrews 4:16?

8. What does 1 Corinthians 10:13 say about temptation?

9. Romans 6:17 says, "Though you were slaves of sin, yet you obeyed from the heart." What does 1 Samuel 15:22–23 say about obedience? What does it say about rebellion?

10. The prodigal son (see Luke 15:11–32), in his search for freedom, became a slave to wrong desires, then he became a slave to wrong deeds, and finally he became a literal slave. Record what James 1:13–16 says about this progression.

_____

_____

_____

_____

_____

11. Recall the heart of the father in dealing with his prodigal son. What did he do, both when his son left home and when he returned home?

_____

_____

_____

God's grace does not give us an excuse to sin but a reason and the provision to obey.

12. According to Romans 6:21, what would be the outcome of the things we did as slaves to sin, things we are now ashamed of, if we did not repent?

_____

_____

_____

_____

Having been set free from sin, you became slaves of righteousness. I speak in human terms because of the weakness of your flesh. For just as you presented your members as slaves of uncleanness, and of lawlessness leading to more lawlessness, so now present your members as slaves of righteousness for holiness. For when you were slaves of sin, you were free in regard to righteousness.

ROMANS 6:18–20

13. Read Romans 6:22–23. What does Romans 6:23 say about the gift we now possess as Christians?

_____

_____

_____

_____

_____

Day 5: Review of Romans 6:1–23

Prayerfully read Romans 6:1–23.

Observe, Interpret, Apply

1. Read the following verses, and answer the questions.

Romans 6:2: What are we are to be dead to?

Romans 6:4: Since "we were buried with Him through baptism into death, that just as Christ was raised from the dead by the glory of the Father," what should we then do?

> You, who once were alienated and enemies in your mind by wicked works, yet now He has reconciled in the body of His flesh through death, to present you holy, and blameless, and above reproach in His sight— if indeed you continue in the faith, grounded and steadfast, and are not moved away from the hope of the gospel which you heard.
>
> COLOSSIANS 1:21–23

Romans 6:8: If we "died with Christ," what do we believe will happen?

2. What fresh insight has this week's study given you regarding the sins of our flesh versus the Spirit of God in us?

3. What is the difference between a believer and a non-believer when it comes to sin?

4. According to 1 John 3:2–5, what does the Bible say about those of us who have our hope in God?

5. Remember 1 John 1:9, and meditate on God's faithfulness!

6. The following three instructions need to be heeded each day we live. Look up the scriptures below, and note what the verse has to say about each instruction.

Romans 6:6: Know:

Romans 6:11: Reckon:

Romans 6:13: Present, or yield:

_____

_____

_____

Our old nature was crucified with Christ, and we constantly have to assert this position of faith. Crucifixion is a slow and tortuous death, as the flesh doesn't die easily. So the two positions of faith we must take are that the old sinful nature is dead and that we're now spiritually alive unto God through Christ.

PASTOR CHUCK SMITH

7. Are you struggling in an area of your life right now? If so, spend some time in prayer, and commit it to Him who is able! Look up Jude 1:24–25, and write the verses here as a thanksgiving for God's ability to work in your life.

_____

_____

_____

_____

_____

Romans 7:1–25

Forbid it, Lord, that I should boast, save in the death of Christ,
my God; All the vain things that charm me most, I sacrifice them to His blood.
Were the whole realms of nature mine, that were an offering far too small;
Love so amazing, so divine, demands my soul, my life, my all.

ISAAC WATTS

Day 1: Overview of Romans 7:1–25

Prayerfully read Romans 7:1–25. This chapter has been prone to misunderstanding and misapplication. We need the Holy Spirit to guide us through His Word, exercising much prayer throughout the study each day. As you read, always remember the context in and purpose for which Paul is writing.

Observe, Interpret, Apply

1. After you prayerfully read Romans 7:1–25, make note of key words or phrases and list them in the chart below, titling each passage and then the chapter.

Vs.	Romans 7:1–6	Vs.	Romans 7:7–14	Vs.	Romans 7:15–25

Passage Title	Passage Title	Passage Title
Chapter Title		

2. Romans 7:1 begins with the word "or," which refers to Romans 6:14: "Sin shall not have dominion over you, for you are not under law but under grace." What does this mean to you?

3. What do you think is Paul's purpose in writing Romans 7?

4. If we are crucified with Christ, what does Romans 7:1 say no longer has dominion over us?

5. What does Paul use as a metaphor about the law in Romans 7:2–3? What point is he trying to make?

6. Summarize in your own words what Paul is saying in Romans 7:4.

7. In the chart below, list the works of our flesh versus the fruit of the Spirit (see Gal. 5:17–26).

Fruit of the Flesh	Fruit of the Spirit

8. Read Galatians 5:16. What are we commanded to do in this verse, and what will happen if we obey?

Day 2: Romans 7:5–9

Walk in the Spirit. That is, walk in fellowship with God. Walk on the spiritual side of your nature. And if you do, you will not be fulfilling the desires of your flesh. The flesh will not be ruling over you anymore. The fleshly desires will not be dominating your life, but your life will be dominated by the Spirit, and thus, by God.

PASTOR CHUCK SMITH

Prayerfully read Romans 7:5–9.

Observe, Interpret, Apply

1. How are sinful passions aroused, according to Romans 7:5?

2. What is the result when we give in to our flesh?

3. Look up the following words from Romans 7:6 using your study tools, and record your findings.

"Delivered" (Strong's #2673):

_____

_____

"Held" (Strong's #2722):

_____

_____

"Newness" (Strong's #2538):

_____

_____

4. Only when we walk in newness of life (in the Spirit) can we serve in the newness of the Spirit. What is the only way we can serve God acceptably? (See Heb. 12:28.)

_____

_____

_____

5. Why would we want to serve in this way, according to Hebrews 12:29?

_____

_____

_____

6. Commit Romans 7:6 to memory this week. Write it out here.

_____

_____

_____

_____

7. Before we can discover the key to Christian living, Paul takes us down the dark path of vanity, flesh, and dependency on the law. If we desire to be delivered from the law, Paul asks the question, "Is the law sin?" Record his answer from Romans 7:7.

8. What is the definition of the law, according to Romans 7:7?

9. As a way of review, look up Galatians 3:24, and record what it says.

10. Look up the following verses, and summarize what they say.

Leviticus 18:1–4:

Deuteronomy 10:12–13:

Psalm 1:1-3:

11. Reread Romans 1:16–20. Paul writes that God is evident in nature, and man is without excuse. Why then is the law even necessary?

> Legalism does not make us more spiritual, it makes us more sinful. Why? Because the law arouses sin in our nature.
>
> WARREN WIERSBE

12. Read the Living Bible's rendering of Romans 7:8-9 below. How does this help you better understand this passage?

> Sin used this law against evil desires by reminding me that such desires are wrong, and arousing all kinds of forbidden desires within me! Only if there were no laws to break would there be no sinning. That is why I felt fine so long as I did not understand what the law really demanded. But when I learned the truth, I realized that I had broken the law and was a sinner, doomed to die.

Day 3: Romans 7:10–14

Prayerfully read Romans 7:10-14.

Observe, Interpret, Apply

1. In Romans 7 the words "I," "me," "my," and "myself" are used fifty-two times. It is important to know that when Paul speaks this way, it is regarding

his old sinful nature. What is true about human nature, according to Romans 7:14?

_____

_____

_____

2. How does Paul describe the believers at Corinth in 1 Corinthians 3:1–4?

1 Corinthians 3:1:

_____

_____

1 Corinthians 3:2:

_____

_____

1 Corinthians 3:3:

_____

_____

1 Corinthians 3:4:

_____

_____

3. Use your study tools to look up the differing definitions for the word "carnal" in 1 Corinthians 3:1–3.

"Carnal" from 1 Corinthians 3:1 (Strong's #4560):

_____

_____

_____

"Carnal" from 1 Corinthians 3:3 (Strong's #4559):

4. What is the significance of the difference between these two meanings?

> Walk in the Spirit, and you shall not fulfill the lust of the flesh.
>
> GALATIANS 5:16

5. For further insight on being a carnal Christian versus a spiritually mature one, read the following excerpt from *Life on the Highest Plane* by Ruth Paxson. Then answer the question below.

The Bible is a mirror in which man may see himself just as he is. Any person who wishes a true picture of himself will find it there. The Bible is God's studio in which will be found the picture of each of His created beings. Your photograph is there. It has been taken by the Divine Photographer, therefore it is flawlessly accurate. Do you wish to see *your* photograph?

The Holy Spirit through the Apostle Paul has divided the human race into three clearly distinguished groups.... God's description of each is so accurate and so true that every person may know with certitude in which class he is.

This classification presents a study of human life on three planes, the lowest, the highest, and a middle plane: or the natural man, the spiritual man, and the carnal man....

The Natural Man

The natural man is without the Lord Jesus Christ as his Saviour, therefore he lives wholly and only unto himself. "The old man" is the centre of his life and has undivided control over his whole being. Self dominates his thoughts, affections, speech, will and actions. His nature is sinful, therefore his conduct is sinful.

The natural man is dead to God but alive to sin, self and Satan. He is under the dominion of the "prince of the power of the air," and is the bondservant of sin. He is a lost man, helpless and hopeless. The tragic part of it is that the "god of this age" has so blinded his mind that he does not comprehend the seriousness of his condition and consequently he has no power within himself to know God, to love God, to receive God, nor even to seek God. Surely this brief sketch of the natural man reveals life lived on the lowest plane. . . .

The Spiritual Man

The spiritual man having taken the crucified, risen, glorified Christ as Saviour, Lord and Life, lives his life wholly unto God. The Lord Jesus is the centre of his life and has undivided control over his whole being.

Jesus Christ dominates his thoughts, affections, speech, will and actions. He has become a partaker of the nature of God so that there are two natures in the spiritual man but the divine nature is sovereign.

The spiritual man is habitually alive to God and dead to sin and self. He is a bondservant to God and gladly, joyously, acknowledges and submits to the sovereign Lordship of Jesus.

Jesus Christ is intensely real and precious to the spiritual man, and he considers, loves, serves, adores and worships Him. This condition is not due to anything within him but is true because of his yielding himself unreservedly to the influence and operation of the Holy Spirit, through whom he has been enabled to see, to receive, to love and to know Christ Jesus as his Saviour and through whom he is filled with His life. Surely this brief sketch of the spiritual man reveals life lived on the highest plane. . . .

The Carnal Man

The carnal man is a Christian because he has obtained sonship through faith in Jesus Christ as his Savior. Therefore he is rightly related to God. But he has entered into neither the possessions nor the privileges of a son and his practices are not those becoming his position in the family of God.

The carnal man has the Holy Spirit dwelling in him but He is constantly being grieved and quenched so that He has restricted power in and dominion over the life.

The carnal man has been renewed through the new birth but he is still a "babe in Christ." He sits at the table of the Lord to partake of His bounties but he has neither appetite nor capacity for "strong meat." He subsists on "milk." He is not a full grown man. He actually has been united to the Lord Jesus but he is an "adulterer" loving the world and caring far more for its people and pleasures than for Jesus Christ (James 4:4).

The carnal man has accepted Christ as his Saviour but he has little or no apprehension of a life of complete surrender to, and of full appropriation of, Jesus Christ as his Lord and his Life. He feels a need of Christ and desires some relationship with Him but he is not satisfied in Him. Christ has *a* place in his heart but not *the* place of supremacy and preeminence. . . .

The carnal man lives his life partly unto God and partly unto himself.

The Lord Jesus is really at the centre of his life but the "old man" is usually on the throne. There is a divided control over his life. Sometimes Christ dominates his thoughts, affections, speech, will and action but more often they are under the dominion of self. Two natures are side by side in the carnal man, the divine and the fleshly, and he is under the sway of each in turn according as he yields to one or to the other. He is alive to God spasmodically but he is equally alive to sin, self and Satan. He attempts to live in two spheres, the heavenly and the earthly, and he fails in both.

The carnal man is in a miserable condition and his life is always one of defeat and discouragement, often one of despair. This condition is due to ignorance of the deep things of God, unwillingness to yield himself unreservedly to the Lord Jesus Christ, and unbelief in appropriating Christ with all His graces. Surely this brief sketch of the carnal man reveals life lived on a middle plane.

We have looked into God's mirror. Have you seen yourself? We have been in God's studio. Have you seen your photograph? We have seen human life on three planes. On which plane are you living?[1]

Simply stated, to be a carnal Christian indicates that Jesus is not Lord of the believer's life but that self-will rules and reigns. Although the Spirit indwells the believer, the flesh masters him. What is the Lord showing you regarding the difference between living under the carnal, or natural, plane and the spiritual plane?

Day 4: Romans 7:15–22

Prayerfully read Romans 7:15-22.

Observe, Interpret, Apply
1. What is the single major difference between the carnal and the spiritual Christian?

2. Why should we choose to live on the highest plane, filled with the Holy Spirit, according to Ephesians 1:12-14?

....

....

....

3. What do the following verses teach about the flesh or the carnal walk?

> You are worthy, O Lord, to receive glory and honor and power; for You created all things, and by Your will they exist and were created.
>
> REVELATION 4:11

Romans 8:7-8: Note which type of carnal Paul is speaking of here:

....

....

....

....

Romans 13:14: What is the antidote for carnality?

....

....

....

2 Corinthians 7:1: What is the motivation to cleanse ourselves from ungodliness?

....

....

....

4. We are all confronted with the question, "Is Jesus Lord of my life?" What fresh insights has God shown you regarding where you stand?

....

....

....

....

167

5. According to Romans 7:18, what stands in the way of a believer keeping the law when the believer tries to do it in his or her own strength?

6. What was present in Paul even when he willed to do good? (See Rom. 7:19–21.) Explain Paul's dilemma (that we all share) in your own words.

7. What did Paul find delight in, according to Romans 7:22?

8. Do you find yourself delighting in the same thing today, or has God's law been a burden to you?

9. Read Jeremiah 17:7–8 below, and underline the blessing we receive when we delight in the Lord.

Blessed is the man who trusts in the LORD, and whose hope is the LORD. For he shall be like a tree planted by the waters, which spreads out its roots by the river, and will not fear when heat comes; but its leaf will be green, and will not be anxious in the year of drought, nor will cease from yielding fruit.

Day 5: Romans 7:23–25

Prayerfully read Romans 7:23-25.

Observe, Interpret, Apply

1. Even though Paul delighted in the law of the Lord, what does he describe in Romans 7:23?

2. Write out Ephesians 6:12 below.

3. What does Ephesians 6:12 mean in practical terms?

4. Where does the battle take place, according to the following verses?

Romans 7:23:

2 Corinthians 11:3:

1 John 2:16:

5. What remedy does the Bible give for this problem in the verses below?

John 15:3–4:

Romans 12:2:

2 Corinthians 10:4–6:

6. How does Satan attack our fleshly nature, according to the following verses?

1 Timothy 4:1–3:

2 Corinthians 11:13–15:

James 1:13–16:

7. What simple twofold instruction does James 4:7 give us as believers?

8. What will be the result of following these two instructions?

9. Write about a time when you felt like Paul when he stated in Romans 7:24, "O wretched man that I am!"

10. Allow Romans 7:25 to encourage you. No believer is exempt from this verse. It has been said that the ground at the foot of the cross is level. What does this mean to you?

_____

_____

_____

_____

_____

_____

11. What has God shown you this week in your study that you did not realize before you began?

_____

_____

_____

_____

_____

Romans 8:1–17

Arise, my soul, arise; shake off thy guilty fears;
The bleeding Sacrifice in my behalf appears:
Before Thy throne my Surety stands, my name is written on His hands.
My God is reconciled; His pardoning voice I hear;
He owns me for His child; I can no longer fear:
With confidence I now draw nigh and "Father, Abba, Father" cry.

CHARLES WESLEY

Day 1: Overview of Romans 8:1–17

Begin your study time with prayer. Then prayerfully reread Romans 7 before reading all of Romans 8. Remember, context rules interpretation, and by rereading Romans 7 you will be able to follow Paul's flow of thought. Note also that Romans 8, as other passages before it, begins with the word "therefore," indicating that it follows on the previous teaching. As you read Romans 8, ask yourself why Paul wrote this chapter.

Romans 6 showed that we are dead to sin and its power over us. Romans 7 showed that we are dead to the law and its authority over us. Now in Romans 8 we will look at the Holy Spirit's work in our lives. Oh, how we need to rely on the finished work of Jesus for everything!

Observe, Interpret, Apply
1. Pull out the key words and phrases from Romans 8:1–17, and list them in the column below; then title the passage. Note that the word "therefore"

in Romans 8:1 is referring to all that has been taught in the previous seven chapters.

Vs.	Romans 8:1-17
Passage Title	

2. Write down any new insight you have gained from Romans 8:1–17.

_____

_____

_____

_____

_____

_____

_____

_____

_____

_____

> It is the presence of the Holy Spirit that the church must seek. He is the help we need, not only in the conflict within the culture in which we live but also in our battle with personal sin and the enticement of the world. We must be filled with the Spirit.

3. Who can claim no condemnation, according to Romans 8:1? In your own words, what does this mean?

_____

_____

_____

_____

_____

4. If you are a believer with the Spirit of God dwelling in you, from where does condemnation come? (See Rev. 12:10.)

> The subject here is no longer Christ's work for us, but the Spirit's work within us.
>
> WILLIAM NEWELL

_____

_____

_____

_____

5. How do believers overcome the enemy's accusations, according to Revelation 12:11?

_____

_____

_____

_____

_____

6. Why did God send His Son? (See John 3:17–18.)

7. Romans 8 contrasts flesh and spirit. Looking only at Romans 8:1–17, list your findings in the columns below.

Vs.	Flesh—Death	Vs.	Spirit—Life

8. Jesus was fully God and fully man. Romans 8:3 says that God sent His only Son in the "likeness of sinful flesh." Using your study tools, look up and write out the definition of the word "likeness" (Strong's #3667).

9. Read Philippians 2:5–11, and note what this passage says about "likeness."

10. What has God done for us? (See 2 Cor. 5:21.)

11. What did Jesus accomplish by coming in the likeness of sinful man, according to Romans 8:3?

12. How does Romans 8:4 tell us the law is fulfilled?

13. Is the law fulfilled in us or by us? What is the difference?

_____

_____

_____

_____

I do not count myself to have apprehended; but one thing I do, forgetting those things which are behind and reaching forward to those things which are ahead, I press toward the goal for the prize of the upward call of God in Christ Jesus. Therefore let us, as many as are mature, have this mind; and if in anything you think otherwise, God will reveal even this to you. Nevertheless, to the degree that we have already attained, let us walk by the same rule, let us be of the same mind.

PHILIPPIANS 3:13–16

14. What does it mean to walk according to the Spirit? (Look up the word "walk" with your study tools to help you answer.)

_____

_____

_____

_____

Digging Deeper (Optional)
Look up the following words from Romans 8:1–4 using your study tools, and write out their definitions.

"Condemnation" (Strong's #2631):

_____

_____

_____

_____

_____

"Walk" (Strong's #4043):

_____

_____

_____

_____

"Free" (Strong's #1659):

Day 2: Romans 8:5–9

Prayerfully read Romans 8:5–9.

Observe, Interpret, Apply
1. What contrast do you find in Romans 8:5–8?

2. Look up "minds" from Romans 8:5 using your study tools, and write out its definition (Strong's #5426).

3. What should our mind-set as believers be, according to the following verses?

    1 Peter 3:8–9:

Philippians 2:3–5:

_____

_____

_____

Philippians 4:8:

_____

_____

_____

4. From the following verses, contrast the final destiny of those persons whose minds are "occupied," or "entertained," by the flesh with those who are occupied with the Spirit.

Philippians 3:18–19:

_____

_____

_____

Colossians 3:1–4:

_____

_____

_____

_____

5. What occupies your mind? If you can honestly say that spiritual things are not on your mind, stop and pray, asking God to give you the mind of Christ.

6. Romans 8:7–8 tells us why those who are in the flesh, or carnally mind-ed, cannot please God. Read these verses from the Living Bible below, and underline the result of continuing to be under the control of your old sinful self:

The old sinful nature within us is against God. It never did obey God's laws and it never will. That's why those who are still under the control of their old sinful selves, bent on following their old evil desires, can never please God.

7. Romans 8:9 gives us a blessed hope! This verse is the key to victory over flesh. Look up the word "dwells" (Strong's #3611) using your study tools, and write out the definition here.

> If we confess our sins, He is faithful and just to forgive us our sins and to cleanse us from all unrighteousness. If we say that we have not sinned, we make Him a liar, and His word is not in us.
>
> 1 JOHN 1:9-10

8. How is it possible for one to dwell on the things of the Spirit? (See Eph. 3:16–20.)

9. Years ago Bob Munger wrote a little booklet called *My Heart, Christ's Home* that told the story of a man and his relationship with Christ. When the man was first saved, his fellowship with the Lord was wonderful, but as time went by, the Lord wanted to clean out the "closets" of this man's life and get rid of things that made his home smell bad and hindered him having close relationship with God. The man struggled to give Christ the key to one particular closet, but when he finally gave up control and let the Lord clean out all the rubbish, he was filled with joy. All of us have locked closets in our hearts. I highly recommend purchasing a copy of this little booklet, *My Heart, Christ's Home* (you can find it at Christianbook.com, www.christianbook.com/my-heart-christs-home-5-pack/robert-munger/9780830865758/pd/65756). As you read it, ask yourself, "Have I given God my key?"

Day 3: Romans 8:10–14

Prayerfully read Romans 8:10-14.

Observe, Interpret, Apply

1. Read Romans 8:10-11. The word "but" always marks a contrast. What does the "but" in verse 10 contrast with?

2. Romans 8:12 marks the conclusion of the previous verses with the word "therefore"; what *is* that conclusion?

3. What does Colossians 1:27 say about "Christ in you"?

4. Who raised Jesus from the dead, according to the verses below?

   John 10:18:

Acts 3:26:

_____

_____

_____

_____

Romans 8:11:

_____

_____

_____

_____

5. What would have happened if Jesus had not risen from the dead?

_____

_____

_____

6. Romans 8:12 says, "Therefore, brethren, we are debtors." What are we to do for God in return for what He has done for us? (See 1 Cor. 6:19–20.)

_____

_____

_____

7. To whom specifically are we debtors, according to Romans 8:12–14?

_____

_____

_____

8. Why are we debtors?

_____

_____

_____

Day 4: Romans 8:14–17

Prayerfully read Romans 8:14–17.

Notice the shift that is occurring here. Paul moves from focusing upon the character of God and his blessings bestowed upon believers, to the responsibilities and obligations that we have in living out the faith. This distinction, however, leads to another distinction. Our obligation does not require us to act on our own, independent of the work of the Spirit within us. It is our faith that must be exercised; we must work out our faith in fear and trembling, but all this is in, by and through the indwelling power of the Holy Spirit.

R. C. SPROUL

Observe, Interpret, Apply

1. What is meant by the phrase "sons of God" in Romans 8:14?

2. Answer the questions from the following verses.

Galatians 3:26: Who are sons of God?

Titus 3:7: How are we justified?

3. What contrast do you find in Romans 8:15?

4. Notice that Romans 8:15 says "the spirit of bondage again to fear." A spirit of fear is something all men are familiar with. List some things that cause you to fear.

_____

_____

_____

_____

_____

5. What is the solution to fear? Note that the kind of fear referred to here is not a reverential fear of God but a negative crippling fear. Look up the following verses, highlighting the one that speaks to your heart the most.

1 John 4:18–19:

_____

_____

_____

2 Timothy 1:7:

_____

_____

_____

Luke 12:7:

_____

_____

_____

Matthew 10:28:

_____

_____

_____

> He Himself has said, "I will never leave you nor forsake you."
>
> HEBREWS 13:5

6. Think about what Romans 8:15–17 means to your life. Not only has God delivered us from the bondage of fear, but also He calls us His children! Write your response to God for what He has done for you.

7. How do you know if you are a son of God? Are you living your life occupied with and speaking about the things of God? The person who is truly led by the Spirit is wrapped up in the things of God, for he is a child of God, rejoicing in and seeking to please his Father in all that he does. Can this be said of you? If not, pray right now and ask God to fill you afresh with His Holy Spirit and give you the mind of Christ.

8. What did Jesus say in John 14:18–21?

9. What can children of God expect as seen in Romans 8:17?

10. Use your study tools to define "suffering" (Strong's #4841).

11. What does it mean to "suffer with Him" (Rom. 8:17)?

12. In what ways did Jesus suffer? Back your answer with Scripture.

13. What did Paul write about suffering, or affliction, in Colossians 1:24?

14. Why do you think Paul could have the perspective he did about suffering?

> Imitate me, just as I
> also imitate Christ.
>
> 1 CORINTHIANS 11:1

Digging Deeper (Optional)

Use your study tools to define the following terms from Romans 8:15.

"Spirit of bondage" (Strong's #1397):

"Fear" (Strong's #5401):

Day 5: Review of Romans 8:1–17

Romans 8 is vital to our walk with God. It begins and ends with incredible encouragements for those who walk in the Spirit.

Observe, Interpret, Apply

1. Reread Romans 8:1–17, and record any fresh insights you gain below.

2. Scripture points out the power of the Holy Spirit in our lives. Find the verse for each statement in the following chart.

Vs.	What the Power of the Holy Spirit Is
8:2–4	The Spirit gives life.
	The Spirit pulls the mind to spiritual things.
	The Spirit dwells within the believer.
	The Spirit gives life to the spirit of the believer.
	The Spirit gives the power to mortify, or put to death, evil deeds.
	The Spirit leads the believer, identifying him as a son of God.
	The Spirit adopts.
	The Spirit bears witness with our spirit.

3. Many in the church today have a distorted view of legalism. When a person says, "I don't drink alcohol," or some such thing, many automatically call him legalistic, when in reality he has come to realize that he is free from fulfilling that particular lust in his life. Freedom in Christ simply means that we are free to do all that is within the parameters of Jesus' life. We are free from the bondage of sin and fear!

True legalism is trying to obtain righteousness by our deeds. Our study in Romans thus far has shown that our righteousness and justification come only by faith in the finished work of Jesus Christ. We cannot add any works to our position in Christ.

When we realize the cost of our position, however, God works a desire in us to be holy as He is holy. Therefore, when we realize the freedom we have from sin in our lives, we are not being legalistic; we are walking in the Spirit and not fulfilling the lustful desires of our flesh. We are free from partaking in sinful or potentially sinful behavior. This is a place in which we will realize the power of God in our lives. Obedience is not legalism! Remember, God has given us grace for obedience (see Rom. 1:5).

What is your definition of legalism? Has your definition changed from before you began your study this week? If so, how?

4. How do you know when you are walking "according to the flesh" (Rom. 8:1)? What is the result?

5. How do you know when you are walking "according to the Spirit" (Rom. 8:1)? What is the result?

6. We often get condemnation confused with conviction. Explain the difference between the two in your own words.

Condemnation:

Conviction:

7. We must refuse condemnation from the enemy but *always* give in to the conviction of the Holy Spirit. He is calling all of us. He has called us with a holy calling! Pray right now that God will continually show you the difference.

The fullness of the Spirit will manifest itself pre-eminently in a supreme consciousness of Christ, an increased holiness of character, and a marked power in service.

OSWALD SANDERS

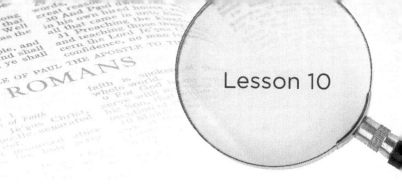
Romans 8:18–39

*We do not lose heart. Even though our outward man
is perishing, yet the inward man is being renewed day by day. For our light
affliction, which is but for a moment, is working for us a far more exceeding
and eternal weight of glory, while we do not look at the things which are seen,
but at the things which are not seen. For the things which are seen are temporary,
but the things which are not seen are eternal.*

2 CORINTHIANS 4:16–18

Day 1: Overview of Romans 8:18–39

Prayerfully read Romans 8:18–39.

Observe, Interpret, Apply

1. As you read Romans 8:18–39, use the chart below to record what Paul
says about the Godhead. You may have to reread the text for each name of
God. This can seem a little redundant, but it will help you establish God's
Word in your heart. Then, at the bottom of the chart, summarize your
findings regarding each person of the Godhead.

God the Father	God the Son	God the Holy Spirit

Summary Statement	Summary Statement	Summary Statement

2. Write out Romans 8:18.

_____

_____

_____

_____

_____

3. What contrast does Paul make between Romans 8:18 and 2 Corinthians 4:17?

_____

_____

_____

_____

4. How does Romans 8:18 change your perspective about trials?

5. Even though we will be grieved in this world by various trials for a little while, what can the result of these trials be when we choose to keep our eyes on Jesus? (See 1 Pet. 1:6-9.)

6. In Romans 8:17-18 Paul speaks of the glory to be revealed in us. What are we instructed to do to realize this glory? (See Col. 3:1-2.)

7. If "your life is hidden with Christ in God" (Col. 3:3), what promise can you claim from Colossians 3:4?

8. Using your study tools, look up the two phrases from Romans 8:19 describing how we are to wait for Christ's appearing. Write out the definition of each.

"Earnest expectation" (Strong's #603):

"Eagerly waits" (Strong's #553):

9. Read Romans 8:19–22 from the Living Bible below. Then ask yourself, "Am I intensely watching in full expectation for the return of Jesus Christ for His church?"

All creation is waiting patiently and hopefully for that future day when God will resurrect his children. For on that day thorns and thistles, sin, death, and decay—the things that overcame the world against its will at God's command—will all disappear, and the world around us will share in the glorious freedom from sin which God's children enjoy. For we know that even the things of nature, like animals and plants, suffer in sickness and death as they await this great event.

Day 2: Romans 8:23

Prayerfully read Romans 8:23.

Observe, Interpret, Apply

1. Who does 1 Corinthians 15:20–23 say is the "firstfruits"?

2. Define "firstfruits" using your study tools (Strong's #536), and write its meaning below.

3. How does James 1:18 describe you as a believer in Jesus as it relates to firstfruits?

> The presence of the Holy Spirit with the believer is the firstfruits of the full harvest of the cross.

4. Romans 8:23 says that we are "eagerly waiting for the adoption, the redemption of our body." Look up the following verses that speak of this event, and record what they say.

1 Corinthians 15:51–58: What is the mystery?

1 Thessalonians 4:13–18: What will happen at the rapture?

1 Thessalonians 5:2–9: How will the rapture take place, and who will be raptured?

Revelation 3:10: What is the purpose of the rapture?

Day 3: Romans 8:24–27

Prayerfully read Romans 8:24-27.

> The greatest problems in my Christian life have come from the weakness of my flesh. Once I experience that glorious metamorphosis, my problems will be over; even so, come quickly Lord Jesus!
>
> PASTOR CHUCK SMITH

Observe, Interpret, Apply

1. Use your study tools to define "patience" (Strong's #5281), and write its meaning below.

2. In Romans 5:3-5 we saw that we are to "glory in tribulations, knowing that tribulation produces perseverance; and perseverance, character; and character, hope. Now hope does not disappoint, because the love of God has been poured out in our hearts by the Holy Spirit who was given to us." According to Hebrews 10:36, why do we need perseverance, or endurance?

3. What must we do to run the race with endurance? (See Heb. 12:1–2.)

_____
_____
_____
_____
_____
_____

4. Write out Philippians 3:13–14 below.

_____
_____
_____
_____
_____

> In the same way—by our faith—the Holy Spirit helps us with our daily problems and in our praying. For we don't even know what we should pray for nor how to pray as we should, but the Holy Spirit prays for us with such feeling that it cannot be expressed in words. And the Father who knows all hearts knows, of course, what the Spirit is saying as he pleads for us in harmony with God's own will.
>
> ROMANS 8:26-27, TLB

5. Who searches the heart and knows the mind of the Spirit, according to Romans 8:27?

_____
_____
_____
_____

6. Underline the words from Psalm 139:1-7 below that minister to you most. Explain why these words speak to you particularly.

O LORD, You have searched me and known me. You know my sitting down and my rising up; You understand my thought afar off. You comprehend my path and my lying down, and are acquainted with all my ways. For there is not a word on my tongue, but behold, O LORD, You know it altogether. You have hedged me behind and before, and laid Your hand upon me. Such knowledge is too wonderful for me; it is high, I cannot attain it. Where can I go from Your Spirit? Or where can I flee from Your presence?

7. When most people quote 1 Corinthians 2:9—"Eye has not seen, nor ear heard, nor have entered into the heart of man the things which God has prepared for those who love Him"—they stop short. What do the next two verses, 1 Corinthians 2:10-11, say that blesses your heart?

Digging Deeper (Optional)

For us to have faith in the ability of God, we need a glimpse of His character. For each attribute of God listed below, look up the verse in which it is found, and summarize the attribute in your own words.

Eternal. The Alpha and Omega, God has no beginning or end. He is outside the time domain! Deuteronomy 32:39-40:

Faithful. God is true to His promises. He cannot lie and is always truthful—He is truth! Deuteronomy 7:9:

Holy. God is a perfect being without sin. All His ways are perfect! Isaiah 57:15:

Immutable. Never changing, God is the same yesterday, today, and forever! Hebrews 13:8:

Incomprehensible. God is beyond man's comprehension. We understand only what God chooses to reveal to us. Romans 11:33:

Infinite. God is limitless. He knows no boundaries! 1 Kings 8:27:

Jealous. God does not share. He alone is worthy of our allegiance! Exodus 34:14:

_____

_____

_____

Just and righteous: God is beyond fair. In Him there is no injustice! Psalm 89:14:

_____

_____

_____

Love. God is love. We cannot love God or one another unless He places His love in our hearts. 1 John 4:7–21:

_____

_____

_____

_____

Omnipotent. God is all-powerful. He need not draw on any source but Himself for His power! Genesis 18:14:

_____

_____

_____

_____

Omnipresent. God is ever-present. He is in all places at all times! Proverbs 15:3:

_____

_____

_____

_____

Omniscient. God is all-knowing. He has perfect knowledge of all things! Psalm 139:1-6:

_____

_____

_____

_____

Wrathful. God hates and punishes all unrighteousness. He will consume all that is against His holiness! Romans 1:18:

_____

_____

_____

What have you learned from this study of the character of God?

_____

_____

_____

Day 4: Romans 8:28-32

Prayerfully read Romans 8:28-32.

Observe, Interpret, Apply

1. Up to this point in Romans, we have been looking at the human will and our willingness to walk in the Spirit—our choice as free moral agents. In Romans 8:28, however, the focus changes completely to God. Once we choose whom we will serve, we can rest in Jesus and no longer focus on ourselves. As Paul said in 1 Corinthians 15:10, "By the grace of *God* I am what I am." In Romans 8 and also in Romans 9, we see the sovereignty of God—meaning that God is totally, supremely, and preeminently over all His creation. Nothing has escaped His control, knowledge, or plan.

After looking up the following verses, choose one, and comment on how it relates to the sovereignty of God.

Romans 8:28–29:

> In Him also we have obtained an inheritance, being predestined according to the purpose of Him who works all things according to the counsel of His will.
>
> EPHESIANS 1:11

1 Corinthians 10:13:

2. Read Romans 8:28. According to this verse, what do we *know*?

3. Who receives the promise of Romans 8:28? Is this verse speaking to a non-believer? Why or why not?

4. Often we quote Romans 8:28 to people when they are going through a trial. We must be careful, however, to whom we quote this verse. It is clear that "all things work together for good," but this promise has a conditional clause. Read this verse in the Living Bible below, and ask yourself if you fit the verse's description. If not, ask God to show you how you can claim this promise.

We know that all that happens to us is working for our good if we love God and are fitting into his plans.

5. Read Romans 8:29-30. Verse 29 takes us from the past, and verse 30 takes us into the future. Using your study tools, define the following terms.

"Foreknew" (Strong's #4267):

_____

_____

_____

_____

"Predestined" (Strong's #4309):

_____

_____

_____

_____

"Called" (Strong's #2822):

_____

_____

_____

_____

6. According to the following verses, when did God choose you?

Ephesians 1:4-5:

_____

_____

_____

_____

2 Timothy 1:9:

_____

_____

_____

_____

Jeremiah 1:5:

_____

_____

_____

_____

"No weapon formed against you shall prosper, and every tongue which rises against you in judgment You shall condemn. This is the heritage of the servants of the LORD, and their righteousness is from Me," says the LORD.

ISAIAH 54:17

7. According to Romans 8:29, to what did God predestine His children?

_____

_____

_____

_____

8. What is the ultimate purpose of God's calling us to Himself, according to Romans 8:30?

_____

_____

_____

9. What questions does Paul ask in Romans 8:31?

_____

_____

_____

10. What is the implied answer to the questions above in Romans 8:32?

_____

_____

_____

11. Who brings charges against us, according to Romans 8:33–34?

_____

_____

_____

12. We know that God is for us, but we also know that Satan is against us. Satan is not God's opposite, nor is he as powerful as our God. How does knowing the attributes of God and that Satan is a created being comfort you today?

_____

_____

_____

_____

13. Read Romans 8:32. The words "freely give" mean to give with no expectation of having the favor returned. This is a picture of God's free gift of grace. God loves you so much that He did not spare His own Son but rather gave Him for you. What does Philippians 4:19 declare?

To Him who is able to keep you from stumbling, and to present you faultless before the presence of His glory with exceeding joy, to God our Savior, who alone is wise, be glory and majesty, dominion and power, both now and forever. Amen.

JUDE 1:24-25

_____

_____

_____

_____

14. How does Matthew 6:25-34 encourage you today?

_____

_____

_____

_____

15. What has God already done for every believer, according to Ephesians 1:3?

_____

_____

_____

_____

Day 5: Romans 8:33–39

Prayerfully read Romans 8:33–39.

> Bless the LORD, O my soul, and forget not all His benefits: who forgives all your iniquities, who heals all your diseases, who redeems your life from destruction, who crowns you with lovingkindness and tender mercies, who satisfies your mouth with good things, so that your youth is renewed like the eagle's.
>
> PSALM 103:2–5

Observe, Interpret, Apply

1. In this passage Paul asks three rhetorical questions. Read those questions in the verses listed here, and answer the questions written below.

Romans 8:33: What does God do?

Romans 8:34: Who is our intercessor?

Romans 8:35: How does Paul respond to the trials of life?

2. Romans 8:36 contains a quote from the Old Testament. Read Psalm 44:22, from which the quote is taken. How does the truth in this verse apply to Paul's previous questions?

3. Romans 8:37 says, "In all these things we are more than conquerors through Him who loved us." Using your study tools, look up the phrase "more than conquerors" (Strong's #5245), and comment.

4. How does the truth of Romans 8:37 speak to you in the circumstances you may be going through?

5. How do the following verses confirm Romans 8:37?

1 Corinthians 15:57:

1 John 5:4–5:

6. From Romans 8:38–39, list the ten things that cannot "separate us from the love of God which is in Christ Jesus our Lord."

> I am persuaded that neither death nor life, nor angels nor principalities nor powers, nor things present nor things to come, nor height nor depth, nor any other created thing, shall be able to separate us from the love of God which is in Christ Jesus our Lord.
>
> ROMANS 8:38–39

7. Can you think of anything that can separate you from the love of God? Use Scripture to support your answer.

> If Christ is in you, no thing will dismay you, but by faith you will overcome the world, the flesh, and the devil. You see, the devil is contending against Omnipotence! Therefore, be steadfast in resisting the evil one, be strong in faith, and give glory to God.
>
> C. H. SPURGEON

8. What do you know from Romans 8:38–39? How should you respond to this truth?

9. What must take place in your life for you to be more spiritually minded and to walk in the victory described in Romans 8? Look for a scripture to support your answer, perhaps something like Proverbs 3:5–7.

_____

_____

_____

_____

_____

_____

_____

_____

_____

_____

The Christian does not work up toward victory, he works down from it. We do not struggle toward it, but we stand in it because of the Cross and an empty tomb. . . . Whatever He [the Holy Spirit] has is held in trust for us, to be bestowed as by faith we claim our inheritance. . . . All of the Lord Jesus Christ is mine at the moment of conversion, but I possess only as much of Him as by faith I claim.

ALAN REDPATH

Romans 9:1–33

O give us hearts to live like Thee, like Thee, O Lord, to grieve
Far more for others' sins than all the wrongs that we receive.

EDWARD DENNY

Day 1: Overview of Romans 9:1–33

In Romans 9 Paul deals with the election of God (His decision to save whomever He will) and the free will of man (our freedom to choose to follow God or not). The discussion of these two seemingly opposite concepts confuses many people. It is important to see the balance that the Bible teaches between the two. Your study this first day will be time consuming, but the time you put into it will be well worth it as you lay the foundation for understanding this truth.

Prayerfully read Romans 9:1–33, keeping in mind that God is sovereign. The Bible clearly teaches both God's sovereign election and man's free choice.

It has been said that these two concepts meet only in the mind of God. But while we do not *comprehend* how these two truths work together, we do *apprehend* them. Because God's Word says they are both true, we know they are. We must just hold onto the truths God shows us and then trust Him for the rest. As Pastor Chuck Smith used to say about things we don't understand, "Stick it in a file labeled 'waiting for further information.'" In the meantime, we should thank God for choosing us and pray, asking God to lead, guide, teach, and fill us with His Holy Spirit.

Observe, Interpret, Apply

1. Using your study tools, write the definitions for the following words; then record their relevance to the corresponding verses. Remember to keep the context of each setting in mind, asking yourself who, what, where, when, why, and how for each word and reference.

"Called" (Strong's #2564):

_____

_____

_____

1 Corinthians 1:9: By whom were you called?

_____

_____

_____

1 Thessalonians 2:12: Why were you called?

_____

_____

_____

"Foreknowledge," or "foreordained" (Strong's #4268):

_____

_____

_____

1 Peter 1:1–2: What do you discover about the "pilgrims of the Dispersion"?

_____

_____

_____

Acts 2:23: What do you learn about Jesus' death?

_____

_____

_____

Romans 8:29: Whom did God predestine, and for what?

"Predestination," or "predestinate" (Strong's #4309):

Romans 8:29–30: Whom has God predestined to be conformed into His image?

Ephesians 1:11: You were predestined according to what?

"Election," or "elect" (Strong's #1589):

John 15:16: What does this say about choice? Why did God choose you?

Romans 8:33: What encourages you from this verse?

2. What new concept or understanding did you gain from today's study?

Day 2: Romans 9:1–13

Prayerfully read Romans 9:1–13.

> These will make war with the Lamb, and the Lamb will overcome them, for He is Lord of lords and King of kings; and those who are with Him are called, chosen, and faithful.
>
> REVELATION 17:14

Observe, Interpret, Apply

1. Read Romans 9:1–5. To what does Paul testify in verses 1–2?

2. Using your study tools, look up "great sorrow" (Strong's 3077) from Romans 9:2, and write its definition below.

3. What is Paul's desire, as expressed in Romans 9:3?

4. What insight does this give you into the love Paul had for his readers?

5. Who are Paul's countrymen, according to Romans 9:3–4?

6. According to Romans 9:4–5, what seven things belong to these chosen people that no others can claim?

7. What truth does Romans 9:5 give about Christ?

8. What statement does Paul make in the first half of Romans 9:6?

9. Note Paul's responses in the following verses.

Romans 9:6:

Romans 9:7 (compare to Genesis 21:12):

Romans 9:8:

10. What does Romans 9:8 say about the "children of the flesh"?

11. The illustration Paul uses of the "children of the flesh" is referring to Ishmael. Ishmael was conceived when Sarah tried to help God fulfill His promise to Abraham by giving her handmaid, Hagar, to Abraham as a wife. But Isaac, not Ishmael, was God's fulfillment of the promise, miraculously born to Sarah in her old age (see Gen. 18:1–15; 21:1–21; Rom. 4:16–22). How does God's free grace given to all for salvation contrast with trying in our own efforts to fulfill God's plan?

12. "Israel" means "governed by God." But not everyone in Israel can say, "I am governed by God." Can you? Why or why not?

13. Read Romans 9:11–13. Keeping in mind the balance between the doctrines we studied on day 1 of this lesson, what are your thoughts?

14. Using your study tools, define "hated" from Romans 9:13 (Strong's #3404), and write its meaning below.

15. How did Jesus use the word "hate" in Luke 14:25–27, and what does this mean for us today?

Digging Deeper (Optional)

Identify someone in the Old Testament who had the type of love for his brethren that Paul had for the Roman believers, and give the scriptural reference.

_____

_____

_____

Why, before Jacob and Esau were ever born, would God accept one and reject the other? The reason is that salvation stands by election alone and not by works. God calls and elects whomever He wishes. So I can't honestly look at myself and say that God elected me because I'm so good. God simply acted on the basis of His own divine sovereignty. The fact that God chose to elect me thrills me and makes me ever grateful to Him! . . . God made His choice in this election with the knowledge that Jacob would be a spiritual man and Esau a fleshly one. Yet no one can say that Jacob was elected because he was so wonderful, kind, or generous. God simply chose him!

PASTOR CHUCK SMITH

Digging Deeper (Optional)

Read Genesis 25:20–28. What distinction did God make between Jacob and Esau?

_____

_____

Read Malachi 1:2–3. Which brother did God favor?

_____

Day 3: Romans 9:14–21

Prayerfully read Romans 9:14–21.

Observe, Interpret, Apply

1. What question did Paul ask in Romans 9:14?

_____

_____

2. What was Paul's answer in the second half of Romans 9:14?

_____

_____

3. What does God say to Moses in Romans 9:15?

4. Read Exodus 33:17–23. What is the context of God's statement to Moses?

5. Why do you think Paul uses this reference to Moses?

6. What is Paul's conclusion in Romans 9:16?

7. Look up the following familiar verses that confirm the concept Paul expresses in Romans 9:16, noting the key words.

John 1:12–13:

John 15:16:

_____

_____

_____

8. In Romans 9:17 Paul speaks of Pharaoh. In Exodus 3:10 we see that God sent Moses to Pharaoh, telling Pharaoh to let God's people go from the land of Egypt. What instruction does God give Moses and Aaron in Exodus 7:1–5?

_____

_____

_____

_____

9. What was the outcome of God hardening Pharaoh's heart, according to Romans 9:17–18?

_____

_____

_____

_____

10. God hardened Pharaoh's heart because Pharaoh had already purposed in his heart to reject God. Look up the following verses, and record what they say about Pharaoh's choice.

Exodus 5:2:

_____

_____

Exodus 8:15:

_____

_____

Exodus 9:34:

11. What have you purposed in your heart regarding God's plan for your life? (See Heb. 3:15.)

12. What is God's basis for predestination as seen in Romans 9:15–16?

13. Summarize the following verses in your own words.

Joshua 24:14–15:

Ezekiel 18:30–32:

John 3:16–18:

> Behold, I stand at the door and knock. If anyone hears My voice and opens the door, I will come in to him and dine with him, and he with Me. To him who overcomes I will grant to sit with Me on My throne, as I also overcame and sat down with My Father on His throne. He who has an ear, let him hear what the Spirit says to the churches.
>
> REVELATION 3:20-22

14. In Romans 9:18 Paul writes, "He has mercy on whom He wills, and whom He wills He hardens." In the Living Bible, Romans 9:19 shows the skeptic's reply to that statement this way: "Well then, why does God blame them for not listening? Haven't they done what he made them do?" How does Paul reply to this in Romans 8:20-21?

_____

_____

_____

_____

_____

_____

_____

_____

15. How do the following verses coincide with Romans 9:20-21?

Isaiah 29:16:

_____

_____

_____

Isaiah 45:9:

_____

_____

_____

Jeremiah 18:4-6:

_____

_____

_____

16. Spend the rest of your time today in prayer. God is God, and if we understood everything about God, _we_ would be God! Just rest in the fact

that He is sovereign and we are not. His ways are not our ways; His ways are higher than our ways (see Isa. 55:8–9).

Day 4: Romans 9:22–24

Prayerfully read Romans 9:22–24.

Observe, Interpret, Apply

1. Some people say things like, "If I am the elect, I will go to heaven, and if I am not the elect, there is no use in my worrying about the way I live my life; it doesn't matter anyway!" What do the following verses indicate about this statement?

Matthew 22:2–3:

> O LORD, You are our Father; we are the clay, and You our potter; and all we are the work of Your hand.
>
> ISAIAH 64:8

2 Peter 3:9:

2. Is the comment in question 1 an accurate statement? Why or why not?

3. What do you think would be a more accurate statement?

4. Read Romans 9:22–24, which speaks of God's sovereignty, in the Living Bible below.

> Does not God have a perfect right to show his fury and power against those who are fit only for destruction, those he has been patient with for all this time? And he has a right to take others such as ourselves, who have been made for pouring the riches of his glory into, whether we are Jews or Gentiles, and to be kind to us so that everyone can see how very great his glory is.

God so loved the world that He gave His only begotten Son, that whoever believes in Him should not perish but have everlasting life. For God did not send His Son into the world to condemn the world, but that the world through Him might be saved.

JOHN 3:16-17

In light of this passage, how should we regard God's patience with us? (See also 2 Pet. 3:9, 15.)

5. What does Ephesians 2:4–10 say about God and why He chose you?

6. What two classes of people does Paul address in Romans 9:22–23?

7. Look up the following words from Romans 9:22 using your study tools, and write out their definitions.

"Wrath" (Strong's #3709):

_____

_____

_____

"Longsuffering" (Strong's #3115):

_____

_____

_____

"Destruction" (Strong's #684):

_____

_____

_____

8. For whom are wrath and destruction reserved?

_____

_____

_____

9. To whom has God shown longsuffering?

_____

_____

_____

10. One challenge in studying Romans is keeping God's sovereignty and man's responsibility in balance. What does 2 Timothy 2:21 say about us as God's vessels and His purpose for us?

_____

_____

_____

_____

Day 5: Romans 9:24–33

Prayerfully read Romans 9:24–33.

> He Himself is the propitiation for our sins, and not for ours only but also for the whole world.
>
> 1 JOHN 2:2

Observe, Interpret, Apply

1. Based on Romans 9:24, whom did God call?

2. Summarize Romans 9:25–28 in your own words below.

3. In Romans 9:29 Paul quotes Isaiah 1:9. (Note: "The LORD of Sabaoth," or "the Lord of hosts," is a title for God. Jehovah Sabaoth emphasizes God's rule over every other power in the material and spiritual universe. This reminds us that all creation, even in its fallen condition, is under God's rule and reign.) What extreme statement did Isaiah make regarding the future of any nation or people that does not have a remnant of those who are faithful to God?

4. Read Romans 9:30–31. What is Paul's conclusion regarding the two groups listed below?

Gentiles:

Israel:

5. How does Romans 9:32 tell us we are to seek righteousness?

6. How does Acts 15:7–11 further elaborate on this?

7. What does Paul mean by a "stumbling stone" in Romans 9:32–33?

8. What does 1 Corinthians 1:23–24 say about this stumbling block?

9. Was there ever a time in your life when the name of Jesus was a stumbling block to you? Explain.

10. Jesus Christ is the Rock! Depending upon our response to Him, He will be to us either a stumbling stone or a foundation stone. Relate the following scriptures with this concept.

Matthew 7:24–25:

Matthew 21:42–44:

Ephesians 2:19–22:

1 Corinthians 10:4:

11. What one thing stood out to you most during your study this week?

On Christ, the solid Rock, I stand; all other ground is sinking sand.

EDWARD MOTE

Romans 10:1–21

It is strange we go on living our everyday lives—
So carelessly, stumbling, dully we plod
Our commonplace paths, and forget that we walk
Every day, every hour, in the presence of God.

MARTHA SNELL NICHOLSON

Day 1: Overview of Romans 10:1–21

Prayerfully read Romans 10:1-21, beginning first with prayer. We need God's guidance and direction as we study His Word. Take time and meditate on each scripture as you read, allowing the Spirit of God to minister to your heart.

Observe, Interpret, Apply
1. As way of review of the book of Romans, fill in the "who" and the "how" in the following chart.

What	Who	How
Sinners	Example: Jews and Greeks, everyone (Romans 3:9, 10, 23)	Example: through Adam (Romans 5:12–19)

What	Who	How
Saved		
Justified		
God's Sovereignty		

2. In Romans 10 Paul shifts his emphasis from God's sovereignty to man's responsibility. While Paul emphasizes Israel in particular, we can find application for our lives as well.

As you read through Romans 10, jot down the reasons Israel rejected faith righteousness in favor of law righteousness:

Romans 10:2:

Romans 10:3:

_____

_____

_____

_____

Romans 10:4–13:

_____

_____

_____

> The LORD looks down from heaven upon the children of men, to see if there are any who understand, who seek God. They have all turned aside, they have together become corrupt; there is none who does good, no, not one.
>
> PSALM 14:2-3

Day 2: Overview of Romans 10:1–21

Prayerfully read Romans 10:1–21.

Observe, Interpret, Apply

1. In Romans 10 Paul quotes the Old Testament ten times. Record Paul's words and then the Old Testament scriptures, each of which speaks of Israel's need for the gospel. Your responses will help you link the Old and New Testaments together.

Romans Reference	Old Testament Reference
Example: Romans 10:5: "Moses writes about the righteousness which is of the law, 'The man who does those things shall live by them.'"	Example: Leviticus 18:5: "You shall therefore keep My statutes and My judgments, which if a man does, he shall live by them: I am the LORD."
Your Response	

Romans 10:6–8:

Deuteronomy 30:12-14:

Your Response

Romans 10:13:

Joel 2:32:

Your Response

Romans 10:16:

Isaiah 53:1:

Your Response

Romans 10:19:	Deuteronomy 32:21:

Your Response

Romans 10:21:	Isaiah 65:2:

Your Response

Day 3: Romans 10:1–8

Prayerfully read Romans 10:1–8.

Observe, Interpret, Apply

1. What does Paul express in Romans 10:1?

Let Your mercy,
O LORD, be upon us,
just as we hope in You.

PSALM 33:22

2. Our hearts are the seat of our wills, thoughts, and emotions. What was Jesus' heart for Jerusalem regarding Israel's rejection of faith righteousness? (See Luke 19:41–42.)

3. According to Romans 10:1, Paul had the heart of Jesus. Do you have this same heart for those who are lost? If not, stop and pray that God would give you His heart for others.

4. Read Romans 10:1–2 and then, using your study tools, look up and write the definition for the word "zeal" (Strong's #2205).

5. The Jewish people had a zeal for God, but is zeal enough for living a godly life?

6. What does Romans 10:3 say about God's righteousness?

7. What did the Jews' zeal cause them to do?

8. What do we see in Paul's life, according to the following verses?

Acts 26:1–11:

Acts 22:3:

Galatians 1:13–14:

9. Zeal is a wonderful thing in the life of a believer. The zeal that Romans 10:3 speaks of, however, resulted in people working out their own righteousness before God. According to Titus 2:11–14, what kind of zeal is God looking for in the believer's life?

10. What should accompany a zealous attitude? (See Rev. 3:19.)

11. What does Romans 10:4 say about the law?

> Are you so foolish? Having begun in the Spirit, are you now being made perfect by the flesh?
>
> GALATIANS 3:3

12. Comment on the meaning of Matthew 5:17.

13. What do you learn about the finished work of Jesus from the following verses?

Galatians 2:19–21:

Ephesians 2:15:

14. What is the contrast between Romans 10:5 and 10:6-8?

> We through the Spirit eagerly wait for the hope of righteousness by faith.
>
> GALATIANS 5:5

Day 4: Romans 10:9–16

Prayerfully read Romans 10:9-16.

Observe, Interpret, Apply

1. According to Romans 10:9-11, what must a man do to be saved?

2. The key word in Romans 10:9-11 is "heart." There is a vast difference between the heart and the head when it comes to spiritual things. How does James 2:14-20 confirm this?

3. Explain the balance between faith and works as expressed in James 2:18.

4. Commit Romans 10:9–10 to memory:

> If you confess with your mouth the Lord Jesus and believe in your
> heart that God has raised Him from the dead, you will be saved.
> For with the heart one believes unto righteousness, and with the
> mouth confession is made unto salvation.

Pastor Chuck Smith says, "Now we come to the matter of human responsibility. Here the truth finds balance. If you confess Him and believe in Him, He will save you because He keeps His Word. 'But what if I am not predestined?' You'll be saved anyhow! No one who has called upon the name of the Lord has been turned away. 'God, be merciful to me a sinner!' (Luke 18:13) is a prayer that has always been answered, for God delights to show mercy. So you're responsible for calling upon the name of the Lord, and when you do, you will be saved!"[1]

5. Who is salvation for, as stated in Romans 10:11–13?

6. What four questions did Paul ask in Romans 10:14–15?

7. Answer these four questions in your own words below.

8. In reflecting on our study, why is the gospel called "the gospel of peace" in Romans 10:15?

> Sing to the LORD, bless His name; proclaim the good news of His salvation from day to day. Declare His glory among the nations, His wonders among all peoples. For the LORD is great and greatly to be praised; He is to be feared above all gods.
>
> PSALM 96:2-4

9. God uses various ways to speak to His people. In some cases He will use a man to preach; in other cases He will use His creation to cry out. God is calling His people to reach out to share the good news of the gospel with a lost and dying world. That is His plan. But He is able to use anything or anyone to bring about His purposes—even a donkey (see Num. 22:22–35).

List a few men and women in the Bible who were obedient to the call God placed on their lives to preach the gospel. Give scriptural references for each.

Day 5: Romans 10:17–21

Prayerfully read Romans 10:17–21.

Observe, Interpret, Apply

1. Read Romans 10:17–21. What passage or concept of the gospel did you hear that caused you to first believe in Christ?

2. According to Romans 10:17, how does faith come?

3. Our faith grows through our study of God's Word and then through seeing it in action as we apply it to our lives. Thank God for working in you "both to will and to do for His good pleasure" (Phil. 2:13)!

4. Record what the following verses reveal about the Word of God.

John 1:14: Who is the Word?

1 Thessalonians 2:13: What does the Word do in those who believe?

Colossians 1:4–6: What does the Word of truth bring forth?

Hebrews 4:12–13: What is the Word like?

Psalm 119:105: How is the Word helpful in your daily walk?

Did they understand that God would give his salvation to others if they refused to take it? Yes, for even back in the time of Moses, God had said that he would make his people jealous and try to wake them up by giving his salvation to the foolish heathen nations. And later on Isaiah said boldly that God would be found by people who weren't even looking for him. In the meantime, he keeps on reaching out his hands to the Jews, but they keep arguing and refusing to come.

ROMANS 10:19–21, TLB

5. Read Psalm 19:1–4: "The heavens declare the glory of God; and the firmament shows His handiwork. Day unto day utters speech, and night unto night reveals knowledge. There is no speech nor language where their voice is not heard. Their line has gone out through all the earth, and their words to the end of the world." What does this passage mean?

_____

6. How does Romans 1:20 confirm Psalm 19:1–4?

If you confess with your mouth the Lord Jesus and believe in your heart that God has raised Him from the dead, you will be saved. For with the heart one believes unto righteousness, and with the mouth confession is made unto salvation.

ROMANS 10:9–10

_____

7. Did anything particularly help you this week as you completed your study?

8. Spend the rest of your study time in prayer for those in your life who have not yet bowed the knee to Jesus.

Romans 11:1–36

They came to the gates of Canaan, but they never entered in;
They came to the very threshold, but they perished in their sin.
Oh, brother, give heed to the warning, and obey His voice today;
The Spirit to thee is calling, oh, do not grieve Him away.
Oh, come in complete surrender, oh, turn from thy doubt and sin;
Pass on from Kadesh to Canaan and a crown and kingdom win.

R. KELSO CARTER

Day 1: Romans 11:1–36

Prayerfully read Romans 11:1–36.

Observe, Interpret, Apply

As you read Romans 11, identify all the verses that deal with the Jews, or Israel, and all those referring to the Gentiles, and note the distinctions between Jew and Gentile in the chart below. Write a summary statement at the bottom of the chart.

Jews, or Israel	Gentiles

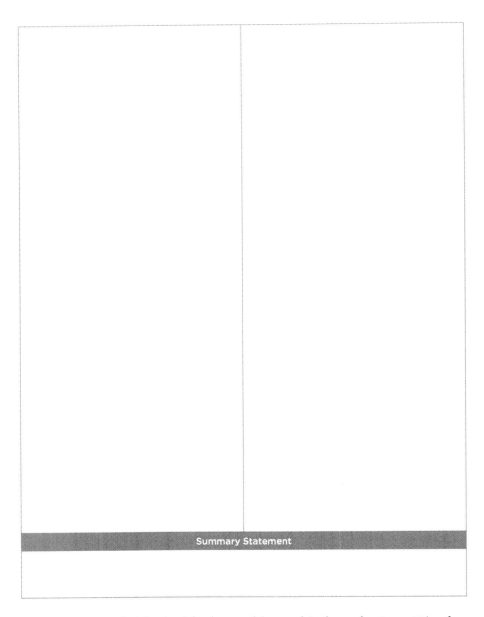

Summary Statement

God is not finished with the world, mankind, or the Jews. His plan has been unfolding throughout history, and great things are still to come! Right now God works individually, bringing men to faith in Jesus Christ. In fact, Paul states that he, being a Jew, personally received Jesus as his Messiah, just as many of his countrymen did.

Currently Israel as a nation has rejected Jesus, but God is not finished with them; in Romans 11 Paul reveals God's unfolding plan for the Jews. God will one day fulfill every promise He has made to Israel when He presents Jesus as their deliverer from Zion. Israel as a nation has been cut off for a time to allow the Gentiles to receive Jesus, but God promises that He will restore Israel to her place. In that day God's people will enjoy great revelation and gladness.

Digging Deeper (Optional)
Divide a piece of paper into three columns. Create column headings reading "Romans 11:1-12," "Romans 11:13-24," and "Romans 11:25-36." List key words and phrases under each heading.

Day 2: Romans 11:1–12

Prayerfully read Romans 11:1–12.

Observe, Interpret, Apply
1. In Romans 11:1 and 11:11, what two questions did Paul ask, and how did he answer each of those questions?

Romans 11:1:

Romans 11:11:

Paul speaks of a "remnant" of Jewish believers in Christ in Romans 11:1–6. His point in asking his first question is to show that he is living proof that God has not cast Israel away completely; He has kept a remnant. Paul was Jewish, yet he chose to follow Christ as Messiah, proving that it is not impossible for a Jew to be saved. His conversion is an example for other Jewish believers.

2. Paul also uses Elijah as an example in explaining the concept of a remnant. Read 1 Kings 19 to see how Elijah, a great prophet although a mere man like you and me, was also one of a remnant in a time of great unbelief. Record your findings below.

3. What characteristic do we see in Elijah in 1 Kings 19:1–10?

4. How did God reveal Himself to Elijah in 1 Kings 19:11–12?

5. As Elijah shifted his focus away from God and onto his circumstances, what does 1 Kings 19:14 tell us was his conclusion?

6. Although Elijah thought he was alone, how many faithful Jews had God preserved in Israel, according to 1 Kings 19:18?

7. Do you ever feel as if you are the only one who is seeking God?

8. Perhaps you have unsaved people in your family or workplace. How does this story encourage you?

> I am accepted by God either wholly by my works or wholly by His grace. I can't be accepted partly by one and partly by the other. If I am accepted by grace then works has nothing to do with my salvation. The good news is that my acceptance is wholly by His grace!
>
> PASTOR CHUCK SMITH

9. What does Isaiah 1:9 say about God's plan for His people?

10. Romans 11:5–6 says, "It is the same today, for a few of the people of Israel have remained faithful because of God's grace—his undeserved kindness in choosing them. And since it is through God's kindness, then it is not by their

good works. For in that case, God's grace would not be what it really is—free and undeserved" (NLT). How does this help you understand grace?

11. Use Ephesians 2:8-9 to confirm what Paul is saying here in Romans 11:1-12.

12. Throughout history God has always had a remnant of believers through which He works. What hope does this give you today?

13. What happened and is continuing to happen to Israel, according to the following verses?

Romans 11:7:

Romans 11:8:

14. Read Romans 11:9-10 in the Living Bible below, and list four things that happened to Israel as a result of seeking salvation by works and not grace.

King David spoke of this same thing when he said, "Let their good food and other blessings trap them into thinking all is well between themselves and God. Let these good things boomerang on them and fall back upon their heads to justly crush them. Let their eyes be dim," he said, "so that they cannot see, and let them walk bent-backed forever with a heavy load."

> Those who know Your name will put their trust in You; for You, LORD, have not forsaken those who seek You.
>
> PSALM 9:10

15. It is not that God does not like certain individuals or is prejudiced in preventing people from coming to Him. Instead, these people experienced the fruit of non-repentant hearts. They chose to seek salvation in their deeds rather than humble themselves and turn to the only One who could save them. They refused God's grace, and therefore God gave them over to the direction in which their hearts were bent. What is your heart bent on today?

Day 3: Romans 11:11–24

Prayerfully read Romans 11:11-24.

Observe, Interpret, Apply
1. Who is Paul speaking to in Romans 11:11–24?

2. What three tragic things happened to the nation of Israel, according to the following verses?

Romans 11:11:

_____

_____

Romans 11:12:

_____

_____

Romans 11:15:

_____

_____

3. Using Romans 11:16–24 as your text, fill in the chart below.

Requirement for Grafting In	Reasons for Branches Being Broken Off

4. Paul used an analogy from nature to explain the salvation of Jews and Gentiles. The natural olive tree represents the Jews, while the wild olive tree represents the Gentiles. What does Romans 11:17 say happened to the Jews who did not believe?

5. As a result, what happened to the wild olive tree (Gentiles), according to the second part of Romans 11:17?

6. Considering this, what did Paul warn the Gentiles in Romans 11:18 *not* to do? And what must the Gentiles remember?

7. Why is it important to guard against an attitude of superiority?

8. According to Romans 11:19, Gentiles can rightly claim that they were "grafted in" because the Jews were "broken off." What did Paul point out about this, however, in Romans 11:20?

9. What warning, therefore, did Paul give in Romans 11:20–21?

10. Use Romans 11:22 to consider and comment on the following concepts.

The goodness of God:

The severity of God:

11. Based on Romans 11:23, what would happen if the unbelieving Jews chose to believe in the grace of God?

12. Compare Romans 11:23 with 2 Corinthians 3:14–16. What do you see?

13. Use Romans 11:24 to explain God's ultimate plan for the Jews' salvation.

14. If you are a Gentile believer, are you thankful to have been "grafted in" by faith in Christ? If so, why?

15. Read about how Jesus summed up this truth in John 15. Based on John 15:5, how dependent should we be on Jesus for our daily living?

> If you abide in Me, and My words abide in you, you will ask what you desire, and it shall be done for you. By this My Father is glorified, that you bear much fruit; so you will be My disciples.
>
> JOHN 15:7-8

16. What happens to us if we refuse to abide in Jesus and are thus unable to bear fruit, according to John 15:6?

17. What does John 15:8 say happens to us if we *do* bear fruit in our lives?

18. Think about John 15:5, and respond to God. Ask Him to show you if you are doing anything in your flesh—if you have failed to abide in Him for His empowering strength to be what He calls you to be. Allow God to speak to your heart, and ask Him for His grace to enable you to bring glory to Him through your situation.

Digging Deeper (Optional)
Read Acts 10, and record below what you learn about the gospel being taken to the Gentiles as a group for the first time.

Day 4: Romans 11:25–32

Prayerfully read Romans 11:25–32.

> Notice how God is both kind and severe. He is very hard on those who disobey, but very good to you if you continue to love and trust him. But if you don't, you too will be cut off.
>
> ROMANS 11:22, TLB

Observe, Interpret, Apply

1. What do you think Paul is referring to when he speaks of the "mystery" in Romans 11:25–26?

2. Using your study tools, define the word "mystery" (Strong's #3466), and write its meaning below.

3. Apply the meaning of "mystery" to Paul's statement in Romans 11:25–26.

4. In Romans 11:26–27 Paul quotes Isaiah 59:20–21 to prove that all Israel will be saved nationally. How will this happen?

5. Compare Paul's statement about Israel's salvation to Zechariah 12:10. What do you see?

6. From Romans 11:27, look up the word "covenant" using your study tools (Strong's #1242), and write its definition below.

7. What is the covenant promise mentioned in Romans 11:27?

8. Paul is speaking of the children of Israel in the context of Romans 11:25–32. What does he mean in Romans 11:29?

9. Look up the following verses, and comment on each one.

Numbers 23:19–20:

John 10:27–30:

10. By way of application to your life today, what does the certainty of God's calling mean to you?

11. This study in Romans is an eye opener for those who think they are good people. Read Romans 11:30–31, and allow it to penetrate your heart. How could this scripture keep you from spiritual pride?

12. Look up 1 Corinthians 10:12, and comment below.

13. In 1 Corinthians 6:9–10 Paul lists people who practice certain lifestyles who will not inherit the kingdom of God. What does he say in verse 11? How is this a humbling thought to you?

14. What does Romans 11:30–32 say about God's mercy?

> He hath shewed thee, O man, what is good; and what doth the LORD require of thee, but to do justly, and to love mercy, and to walk humbly with thy God?
>
> MICAH 6:8, KJV

15. When you find it difficult to show mercy to others, how does 2 Peter 1:3–4 help you?

Day 5: Romans 11:33–36

Prayerfully read Romans 11:33–36. For better clarity and understanding, read the passage in several versions, if you have access to them.

Observe, Interpret, Apply

1. How do the following verses amplify what Paul is saying in Romans 11:33–36?

Ecclesiastes 3:11:

Isaiah 55:8:

Ephesians 3:19:

2. While God's ways are past finding out, what does 1 Corinthians 2:16 say about believers in Jesus?

3. Having the mind of Christ does not mean understanding God and His ways perfectly, but it does mean that God has revealed Himself and His truth to believers—enough of Himself and His ways to save us from sin, death, judgment, and hell. Though God is unsearchable and His ways are past finding out, Jesus "endured the cross, despising the shame," . . . "for the joy that was set before Him" (Heb. 12:2). That joy was a relationship with you and me, and through Jesus we can know God in intimate relationship. What does it mean to you to know God?

4. What are some truths you can learn from Paul's example of the pursuit of knowing God?

Galatians 4:8–9:

Ephesians 1:16–23:

5. As Paul considered God's plans, he broke into praise. What did he exclaim about God in Romans 11:33?

6. In Romans 11:34–35 Paul used Isaiah 40:13 and Jeremiah 23:18 to affirm God's wisdom. Take a moment to write your own expression of praise concerning God's wisdom.

7. What warnings should you heed in your life from Romans 11?

THE POWER OF THE GOSPEL

> We know that the Son of God has come and has given us an understanding, that we may know Him who is true; and we are in Him who is true, in His Son Jesus Christ. This is the true God and eternal life.
>
> 1 JOHN 5:20

8. From your study this week, which example, Paul or Elijah, do you most desire to follow?

_____

_____

_____

_____

_____

_____

_____

Romans 12:1–21

My glorious Victor, Prince Divine,
Clasp these surrendered hands in Thine;
At length my will is all Thine own,
Glad vassal of a Savior's throne.

H. C. G. MOULE

Day 1: Romans 12:1–2

Prayerfully read Roman 12:1–2.

Observe, Interpret, Apply

1. Thus far in the book of Romans, Paul has four times used the word "therefore" to begin a statement. List what follows each statement in the verses below.

Romans 3:20:

Romans 5:1:

Romans 8:1:

_____
_____
_____
_____

Romans 12:1–2:

_____
_____
_____
_____

2. Define the following words, using your study tools.

"Holy" (Strong's #40):

_____
_____
_____
_____

"Acceptable" (Strong's #2101):

_____
_____
_____
_____

3. What is Paul calling us to do in Romans 12:1–2?

_____
_____
_____

4. How does Romans 12:1 say we can do this?

_____
_____

5. Is there anything we can do or offer to God on our own that would be pleasing to Him?

6. How does Hebrews 12:28 reinforce this truth?

7. Explain in your own words how we can present our bodies as living sacrifices to God.

8. Is there a difference in your life since you have come to know Christ as your Lord and Savior? Did you use your body or mind in a way before you knew Christ that differs from how you live today? Do you have a testimony of what God saved you from? Either way, think about it, and pray that God continues to sanctify you (set you apart for His service).

9. Read 1 John 1:8–10, remembering that we were all born into sin. No one's sin is worse than another's. In God's eyes sin is sin. Respond to this truth below.

10. Why would you present yourself holy and acceptable to God, according to Hebrews 10:19–23?

_____

_____

_____

> I do not count myself to
> have apprehended; but
> one thing I do, forgetting
> those things which are
> behind and reaching
> forward to those things
> which are ahead, I press
> toward the goal for the
> prize of the upward call of
> God in Christ Jesus.
>
> PHILIPPIANS 3:13–14

11. Write out Romans 12:1–2, and commit it to memory.

_____

_____

_____

_____

_____

_____

_____

12. In *The Gospel According to Grace*, Pastor Chuck Smith wrote,

> Many people seek to relate man to animals because they want to live like them. Animals do not possess a spirit and live solely on a body conscience level. So the man wants to feel free of any responsibility to God. He disclaims his spiritual capacity and proclaims himself a highly evolved animal. He's constantly searching for the missing link between himself and the ape. Natural man does have a missing link, but it is not between man and the animal kingdom, it is between man and God. Man once created in the image of God has fallen from the Spirit-controlled being he once was to the flesh-controlled being he has become. Now God seeks to restore man into His image by the new birth.[1]

How do we transform (cleanse) our minds from this natural way of thinking, according to the following verses?

Ephesians 5:26:

_____

_____

_____

Titus 3:5–7:

_____

_____

_____

Ezekiel 36:25–27:

_____

_____

_____

Take my life and let it be
Consecrated, Lord, to Thee.
Take my hands and let them move
At the impulse of Thy love.
Take my feet and let them be
Swift and beautiful for Thee.
Take my voice and let me sing
Always, only, for my King.

FRANCES RIDLEY HAVERGAL

13. Spend some time in prayer meditating on the above verses. How has God opened your heart to these insights?

_____

_____

Digging Deeper (Optional)
Divide a piece of paper into three columns, and head the columns with "Romans 12:1–8," "Romans 12:9–13," and "Romans 12:14–21." List all the key words and phrases from these passages, and title each section.

Day 2: Romans 12:3–8

Prayerfully read Romans 12:3–8.

Observe, Interpret, Apply
1. Throughout the study of Romans, we have looked at the grace of God from many different angles. This subject is crucial to our Christian walk.

The life we now live in Christ is only by the grace of God. When we understand what we have studied thus far—that there is none righteous, no not one—we gain a proper perspective on who we are. By way of review, look up the following scriptures, and comment on each one.

Romans 12:3:

_____

_____

_____

Philippians 2:3–8:

_____

_____

_____

1 Corinthians 15:10–11 (Paul's personal testimony):

_____

_____

_____

2. What metaphor for the family of God does Paul use in Romans 12:4–5?

_____

_____

_____

_____

3. Paul seems to switch gears here in Romans 12 to talk about spiritual gifts. He is not really changing the subject, however, as he moves from talking about mercy and grace and humility to "a measure of faith" (Rom. 12:3), because his emphasis here is not on the gifts themselves but on the attitudes in which the gifts are to be exercised. According to the following scriptures, how we are to conduct ourselves as members of the body of Christ?

1 Corinthians 13:1–2: What is necessary?

Galatians 5:22–26: How will we know if what we do is powered by God?

> Since you are zealous for spiritual gifts, let it be for the edification of the church that you seek to excel.
>
> 1 CORINTHIANS 14:12

4. Four major sections of Scripture deal with spiritual gifts. List in the chart below what you learn about spiritual gifts from the following passages.

Romans 12:4-8	1 Peter 4:10-11	1 Corinthians 12:1-31	Ephesians 4:1-16

Day 3: Romans 12:9–16

Prayerfully read Romans 12:9-16.

Observe, Interpret, Apply

1. Paul lists many contrasts in this section of Scripture. In the chart below identify which attitudes and actions should and should not affect our behavior, as stated in Romans 12:9–21.

What We Should Do	What We Should Not Do

2. Write Romans 12:9 in your own words below.

3. How does Psalm 101:3 reiterate Romans 12:9?

4. From Romans 12:11, use your study tools to look up the following words, and write their definitions below.

"Lagging" (Strong's #3636):

"Diligence" (Strong's #4710):

"Fervent" (Strong's #2204):

"Spirit" (Strong's #4151):

5. Comment on the following scriptures regarding our attitudes and behaviors.

Proverbs 13:4:

2 Thessalonians 3:6–12:

6. How does the teaching in Romans 12:12 go against our natural tendency?

7. Look up in your study tools the following words from Romans 12:12. Write their definitions below; then answer the question pertaining to each word.

"Hope" (Strong's #1680):

What is our hope? (See Col. 1:27.)

"Patient" (Strong's #5278):

What helps us be patient? (See 1 Thess. 1:3–4.)

"Tribulation" (Strong's #2347):

How can we glory in our tribulations? (See Rom. 5:3–5.)

> The righteousness of God apart from the law is revealed, . . . even the righteousness of God, through faith in Jesus Christ, to all and on all who believe.
>
> ROMANS 3:21–22

8. What does Romans 12:15 say about our responses to others?

9. Whose heart must we have for others for us to be able to respond to them as we should?

10. Only if we do not think too highly of ourselves will we be able to weep with those who weep and rejoice with those who rejoice. Write a prayer asking God to give you His heart for others.

> This is My commandment, that you love one another as I have loved you. Greater love has no one than this, than to lay down one's life for his friends.
>
> JOHN 15:12–1

Day 4: Romans 12:16–21

Prayerfully read Romans 12:16–21.

Observe, Interpret, Apply

1. Paul addresses how we are to deal with those who are alienated or having conflicts with us. From the following verses, summarize how we are to react when dealing with difficult people.

Romans 12:16:

Read and meditate on Philippians 2:1–8.

Romans 12:17:

Read and meditate on 1 Peter 3:8–9.

Romans 12:18:

Read and meditate on Hebrews 12:14.

Romans 12:19:

_____

Read and meditate on Leviticus 19:18.

Romans 12:20:

_____

_____

_____

> Do you despise the riches of His goodness, forbearance, and longsuffering, not knowing that the goodness of God leads you to repentance?
>
> ROMANS 2:4

2. What principle does Paul give in Romans 12:21 that applies not only to dealing with difficult people but also with our own sinful nature?

_____

_____

_____

Day 5: Review of Romans 12:1–21

Prayerfully read Romans 12:1–21.

Observe, Interpret, Apply

1. Note the exhortations of Romans 12:9–21 that reflect the lifestyle of a "living sacrifice" (Rom. 12:1) to God. Since we *are* living sacrifices by the grace of God, serving Him with the spiritual gifts He distributes to each of us as He wills, what should our behavior look like, according to Romans 12:9–21?

Romans 12:9:

_____

_____

_____

Romans 12:10:

Romans 12:11:

Romans 12:12:

Romans 12:13:

Romans 12:14:

Romans 12:15:

Romans 12:16:

Romans 12:17:

Romans 12:18:

Romans 12:19:

Romans 12:20:

Romans 12:21:

2. Which verse in the list above stood out to you as an area that needs the most work in your life?

3. From your study this week, share what spoke to you most regarding the following topics.

Love and humility:

Fellowship:

Your enemies:

4. We all fall short continually, but God will be faithful to complete the work He began in each one of us. Spend some time today thanking Him that you can be confident of this very thing: "He who has begun a good work in you will complete it until the day of Jesus Christ" (Phil. 1:6).

The righteousness of God apart from the law is revealed, . . . even the righteousness of God, through faith in Jesus Christ, to all and on all who believe.

ROMANS 3:21–22

Romans 13:1–14

It is not enough to own a Bible; we must read it.
It is not enough to read it; we must let it speak to us. It is not enough to let it speak
to us; we must believe it. It is not enough to believe it; we must live it.

WILLIAM A. WARD

Day 1: Overview of Romans 13:1–14

Prayerfully read Romans 13:1–14.

Observe, Interpret, Apply

1. As you begin your day in prayer, does anything stand out to you from last week's lesson? If so, share it below.

_____

_____

_____

2. Has anything prevented you from presenting yourself to God as a living sacrifice this week? If so, what?

_____

_____

_____

3. Our relationships with others are a reflection of our relationship with God. As we obey Romans 12:1-2, how do you think our relationship with others will be affected?

4. What example did God set for us in Romans 5:8 when we were "difficult"?

5. Prayerfully read all of Romans 13 in one sitting. Then read it a second time, and note any fresh insight God gives you. Keep in mind that when Paul wrote this epistle to the believers in Rome, Nero was the reigning emperor. He was cruel, sadistic, and deranged. Nero lived a life of debauchery, murdering scores of innocent people, including Christians. Ultimately, he would be responsible for the apostle Paul's murder. In light of this, why was Paul's exhortation concerning the governing authorities remarkable?

6. If you had to give Romans 13 one title, what would it be?

7. Many Christians have debated over the centuries what the relationship between the believer and the state should be. Which is supreme, they wonder, the church or the state? God pulls no punches in dealing with the issue in Romans 13, and what He says to the genuine believer is startling to some.

Simply stated, God expects believers to live as a testimony of righteousness by doing what is right as citizens of this earth in the midst of evil. Define the following words using your study tools, and write the meanings below.

"Be subject" (Strong's #5293):

_____

_____

_____

"Appointed," or "ordained" (Strong's #5021):

_____

_____

_____

8. Read Romans 13:1-7. In this passage Paul continues the thought of a believer as a living sacrifice and gives practical exhortation about what our conduct should be. Use the chart below to identify his message about each topic listed.

Governing Authorities	Our Consequences	Application for Our Lives

9. According to Romans 13:1–7, what three things does Paul list as the purpose of government?

Romans 13:1–2:

Romans 13:3–5:

Romans 13:6–7:

10. Submission to the government can be a difficult concept to accept, since wrong is becoming increasingly considered right in our society. According to Romans 1:5, what provision has God given us for obeying our leaders?

11. It is often difficult to obey governing authorities when they are corrupt. Who is in control, regardless of how things appear? (See Prov. 21:1.)

12. Read 1 Peter 2:13-17. What are we instructed to do?

13. What will be the result of our obedience to this command of God through Peter?

14. While we are free, what does 1 Peter 2:16 say we are in Christ?

15. Besides addressing our attitude toward government, what else does Peter instruct us to do?

16. As believers, we must be careful to consider our own responsibility to obey and not give excuses for disobedience. What does Romans 14:12 say about accountability?

17. According to Romans 13:3, what can you do to keep from living in fear of the authorities?

_____

_____

_____

> That obedience which is not voluntary is disobedience, for the Lord looketh at the heart, and if He seeth that we serve Him from force, and not because we love Him, He will reject our offering.
>
> C. H. SPURGEON

Digging Deeper (Optional)

What did Jesus tell His disciples about paying taxes? (See Mark 12:15–17.)

_____

_____

_____

_____

_____

Some Christians argue that we should not pay taxes. Do you see any scriptural basis against paying taxes? If so, give the reference.

_____

_____

_____

In obedience to Philippians 4:8, list some good things that come from our tax dollars, and praise God for them!

_____

_____

_____

Day 2: Romans 13:1–7

Prayerfully read Romans 13:1–7. For further understanding, read the passage in the Living Bible below:

Obey the government, for God is the one who has put it there. There is no government anywhere that God has not placed in power. So those who refuse to obey the laws of the land are refusing to obey God, and punishment will follow. For the policeman does not frighten people who are doing right; but those doing evil will always fear him. So if you don't want to be afraid, keep the laws and you will get along well. The policeman is sent by God to help you. But if you are doing something wrong, of course you should be afraid, for he will have you punished. He is sent by God for that very purpose. Obey the laws, then, for two reasons: first, to keep from being punished, and second, just because you know you should.

Pay your taxes too, for these same two reasons. For government workers need to be paid so that they can keep on doing God's work, serving you. Pay everyone whatever he ought to have: pay your taxes and import duties gladly, obey those over you, and give honor and respect to all those to whom it is due.

Observe, Interpret, Apply

1. The apostle Paul is telling us in Romans 13:1-7 to obey the authorities that are placed over us. Relate his comments with Matthew 28:18.

2. Though we are to obey the governing authorities, what are the exceptions to obeying them? (See Acts 5:29.)

3. Noah and Lot (see Gen. 6:5-12; 19:1-11) knew what it meant to submit to governing authorities in wicked and godless societies. How does Peter

encourage you in 2 Peter 2:9, since we too are called to submit to worldly governing authorities?

4. Look up the following scriptures written by Peter and Paul, who were both eventually killed for their faith by the very government they were telling Christians to obey. What did they have to say about governing authorities?

1 Timothy 2:1–2:

1 Peter 2:13–17:

5. List the authorities that are placed over you today.

6. What is the result when we resist authority, according to Romans 13:2?

7. What do you think keeps us from wanting to obey those in authority over us?

8. What should you do when you do not agree with the authorities placed over you?

> He Himself has said, "I will never leave you nor forsake you." So we may boldly say: "The LORD is my helper; I will not fear. What can man do to me?"
>
> HEBREWS 13:5–6

9. What does Paul say in Colossians 4:1 that helps our perspective as believers?

Digging Deeper (Optional)
Read Daniel 3. Then, on a sheet of paper, list the order of events in this chapter, who was involved in those events, and what you know about each person. What do you learn about submitting to God from this chapter?

Day 3: Romans 13:8–10

Prayerfully read Romans 13:1–10, reviewing yesterday's passage as it applies to today's.

Observe, Interpret, Apply

1. According to Romans 13:8, what is our debt as Christians? Why?

2. Using your study tools, define the following words, and write their meanings below.

"Love" (Strong's #25):

"Fulfilled" (Strong's #4137):

3. How do these definitions minister to you as you think about what love results in?

4. What is the new commandment Christ gave us in John 13:34?

5. What will be the result of obeying this commandment, based on John 13:35?

6. What instructions does Paul give us in Galatians 5:13–16?

7. Ultimately, what do our Christian lives boil down to?

8. Sum up the law of God in one word.

9. Look up the following passages, and list below them what they have to say about love. Then write a summary statement for each passage.

Romans 13:8–10	1 John 4:7–21	1 Corinthians 13

Summary Statement	Summary Statement	Summary Statement

10. Take some time to allow God to speak to you about what you have studied today. What impressed you most?

_____

_____

_____

_____

Day 4: Romans 13:11–14

Prayerfully read Romans 13:11–14.

Observe, Interpret, Apply
1. Write out Romans 13:11–14 below.

_____

_____

·····

2. How does Matthew 24:42–51 relate to Romans 13?

·····

> Owe no one anything except to love one another, for he who loves another has fulfilled the law.
>
> ROMANS 13:8

3. What does 1 Thessalonians 5:1–6 say about us as Christians being the "children of light" (KJV)?

·····

> You, beloved, building yourselves up on your most holy faith, praying in the Holy Spirit, keep yourselves in the love of God, looking for the mercy of our Lord Jesus Christ unto eternal life.
>
> JUDE 1:20–21

4. Fill in the chart below, using Ephesians 5:11–18.

What We Are to Do	What We Are Not to Do
Ephesians 5:11:	Ephesians 5:11:
Ephesians 5:14:	Ephesians 5:12:
Ephesians 5:15:	Ephesians 5:17:
Ephesians 5:17:	Ephesians 5:18:

5. How would living a Romans 12:1-2 life sum up today's scripture references?

6. What are some things that could be considered the "works of darkness" (Rom. 13:12), according to the Word of God?

7. What is the "armor of light" spoken of in Romans 13:12? Use your study tools to help you answer.

"Armor" (Strong's #3696):

"Light" (Strong's #5457)

8. Look up the following words that Paul uses in Romans 13:13 that identify what we are to cast off. Write their definitions below.

"Revelry" (Strong's #2970):

"Drunkenness" (Strong's #3178):

"Lewdness," or "chambering" (Strong's #2845):

"Lust," or "wantonness" (Strong's #766):

"Strife" (Strong's #2054):

"Envy" (Strong's #2205):

> The free gift of eternal salvation is now being offered to everyone; and along with this gift comes the realization that God wants us to turn from godless living and sinful pleasures and to live good, God-fearing lives day after day, looking forward to that wonderful time we've been expecting, when his glory shall be seen—the glory of our great God and Savior Jesus Christ.
>
> TITUS 2:11-13, TLB

Day 5: Review of Romans 13:1-14

Prayerfully read Romans 13:1-14.

Observe, Interpret, Apply
1. Read 1 Peter 2:11-18. What word does Peter use to address believers at the beginning of verse 11? What two words does he use to describe believers in the same verse?

2. What will be the result if we abstain from fleshly lusts, according to 1 Peter 2:12?

3. Based on 1 Peter 2:13–15, to whom are we to submit, and why?

4. How does Peter describe us in 1 Peter 2:16?

5. How could we use liberty as a "cloak for vice" (1 Pet. 2:16)?

6. What five things does Peter call us to do as believers in 1 Peter 2:17–18?

7. Read James 1:13–15. Who is the one tempting us with sin?

8. Where does desire begin, according to James 1:14?

9. What does James 1:15 say happens when our desire has conceived?

10. What does sin ultimately produce, based on James 1:15?

11. Are you entertaining a sin or something not pleasing to God in your mind or heart? If so, lay it at the cross of Jesus through prayer!

12. How would hiding Galatians 2:20 in your heart help you "make no provision for the flesh" (Rom. 13:14)?

The church today is suffering from the secularization of the sacred. By accepting the world's values, thinking its thoughts and adopting its ways we have dimmed the glory that shines overhead. We have not been able to bring earth to the judgment of heaven so we have brought heaven to the judgment of the earth. Pity us, Lord, for we know not what we do!

A. W. TOZER

13. Can you say with Paul that you always strive to have a blameless conscience before God and man (see Acts 24:16)? What are some ways you need to change in this area?

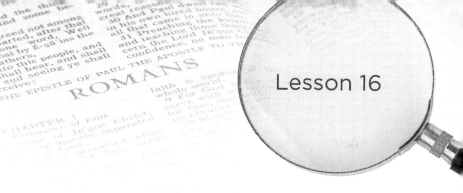

Romans 14:1–23

Many times Christians base their moral judgments
on opinion, personal dislikes, or cultural bias rather than on the Word of God.

LIFE APPLICATION NEW TESTAMENT COMMENTARY

Day 1: Overview of Romans 14:1–23

Prayerfully read Romans 14:1–23, asking God to reveal new insights to your heart.

Observe, Interpret, Apply

1. Read Romans 14:1–23 two more times—once to pull out the facts about those who are weak and once to pull out the facts about those who are strong. List your findings below.

The Weak	The Strong

The Weak	The Strong

2. The issue of Christian liberty versus license always confronts believers (and the church) as we desire to please our Lord. So often people ask, "What can a believer do or not do socially and personally?" How do you answer this question for your own life?

_____

_____

_____

_____

_____

3. In Romans 14 Paul stresses that we are to avoid pointless divisions over matters of conscience that are not specific commands of Scripture. What is the one thing we need in order to overlook others' convictions or lack of them? Reread Romans 13:8-10 to help you answer.

_____

_____

_____

_____

_____

_____

Paul, in chapter fourteen and fifteen of the book of Romans, directs his instruction chiefly "to the strong," who can bear it, while indirectly showing the state of the "weak." Those weak in faith, like babes, are not able to take much nourishment at once; while those who are strong are often not willing to receive what seems to reflect upon their vigor. To have faith before God, secretly, hiding it from the weaker brother, for his sake, until he becomes stronger, is not easy: it requires walking in God's love, which is always costly to the one loving!

WILLIAM R. NEWELL

Day 2: Romans 14:1–6

Prayerfully read Romans 14:1–6. As you continue your study of Romans, keep in mind that our righteousness does not come by what we do, but rather Christ's righteousness is imputed to us by what He alone has done—righteousness comes solely by His grace! Allow the Spirit to minister to your heart with fresh insights.

Observe, Interpret, Apply

1. Using your study tools, look up the following words from Romans 14:1, and record their definitions below.

"Receive" (Strong's #4355):

"Disputes," or "disputations" (Strong's #1253):

"Doubtful" (Strong's #1261):

2. According to Romans 14:1–6, what attitude are we to have toward other believers, whether they are mature Christians or babes in Christ?

3. Record below what 1 Corinthians 8:1 says.

4. Remember that the church in Rome consisted of Jewish believers and Gentiles, just as the church today is filled with people from various religious

and cultural backgrounds. Paul's point in addressing the church at Rome was to get them not to overlook habitual sin but to overlook petty differences. Record what Paul says in 1 Corinthians 13:7 about the result of God's love.

_____

_____

_____

_____

5. Colossians sums up this attitude perfectly. Read Colossians 2:9–13. What does verse 9 say that we are in Christ?

_____

_____

_____

_____

6. According to Colossians 2:12–13, what is the benefit of being found in Christ?

_____

_____

_____

_____

> I also count all things loss for the excellence of the knowledge of Christ Jesus my Lord, for whom I have suffered the loss of all things, and count them as rubbish, that I may gain Christ and be found in Him, not having my own righteousness, which is from the law, but that which is through faith in Christ, the righteousness which is from God by faith; that I may know Him and the power of His resurrection, and the fellowship of His sufferings, being conformed to His death, if, by any means, I may attain to the resurrection from the dead.
>
> PHILIPPIANS 3:8–11

Day 3: Romans 14:7–13

Prayerfully read Romans 14:7–13.

Observe, Interpret, Apply
1. What insights did God show you as you read Romans 14:7–13?

_____

_____

_____

_____

2. Look up the following scriptures, and comment on each one.

1 Corinthians 6:19–20:

Matthew 16:25–26:

Galatians 2:20:

3. According to Romans 14:9, why did Christ die?

4. What should be our response to Him, based on Romans 14:7–8?

5. Even though God is Lord of all and the righteous judge, what trap does the church fall into as stated in Romans 14:10?

6. Romans 14:10–12 tells us why this is wrong. What does it say?

> We all have an influence on other people. We don't live in isolation chambers.
>
> PASTOR CHUCK SMITH

7. Judgment leads to condemnation. Referring back to Romans 8:1, where does condemnation come from?

8. Who is condemned? (See John 3:18.)

9. What does John 5:24 say about the believer regarding judgment?

10. Look up the following scriptures that tell of the judgment reserved for non-believers leading to condemnation, and answer the related questions.

Revelation 20:11: What is this judgment called?

Revelation 20:11–14: What will happen at this final judgment for non-believers?

Revelation 20:15: What is the end for the non-believer?

11. A second judgment spoken of in the Bible is for believers only, and it is referred to as the judgment seat of Christ. Paul mentions this in 2 Corinthians 5:10, referring to the Greek *bema* (Strong's #968), a place where athletic games were judged and rewards handed out at the end of a contest. What do the following verses say about this judgment that is for believers only?

1 Corinthians 3:11–15: What will be judged?

2 Corinthians 5:9–11: Who will be judged?

12. How can our works survive the fire of judgment? Look up Matthew 6:1–5 to help you answer.

13. We are not to serve with the goal of getting a reward. We serve God in response to what He has done for us. Read Revelation 4:10–11, and record what the twenty-four elders (who represent the church) do with the crowns they receive.

_____

_____

_____

> Since we are receiving a kingdom which cannot be shaken, let us have grace, by which we may serve God acceptably with reverence and godly fear. For our God is a consuming fire.
>
> HEBREWS 12:28-29

14. In light of all you have studied today, what perspective does the Lord desire His children to have, according to the following scriptures?

1 Corinthians 9:24–27:

_____

_____

_____

Hebrews 12:1–2:

_____

_____

_____

Philippians 3:14:

_____

_____

_____

Day 4: Romans 14:14–20

Prayerfully read Romans 14:14–20.

Observe, Interpret, Apply
1. Use your study tools to look up the following words from Romans 14:14–17, and write their definitions below.

"Convinced," or "persuaded" (Strong's #3982):

"Unclean" (Strong's #2839):

"Grieved" (Strong's #3076):

2. In a pagan sacrifice, only a portion of the animal was offered, and the remainder was eaten by the worshipers or sold in the market alongside other meat. The Jews began to inquire whether it was lawful to eat this meat because of a command in the law from Exodus 34:15. Read Acts 10:9–16. What does God say about eating that which is unclean (offered to idols)?

3. What instruction is given in 1 Timothy 4:4?

4. What makes a man unclean? (See Matt. 15:17–20.)

5. In Romans 14:15, what admonition is given to a person who grieves his brother by his actions?

6. Comment on Paul's exhortation to us as Christians in 1 Corinthians 10:31–33.

7. According to Romans 14:17, what three things does the kingdom of God consist of?

8. How do we access these three things?

9. What is the kingdom of God *not*, based on Romans 14:17?

10. Whom does Romans 14:18 say we are serving?

11. As stated in Romans 14:19, what are we to pursue?

> You can do a right thing in a wrong way. Your actions may be all right, but you can do it offensively, and that is an act of evil. You are destroying the work of Christ in a person instead of building him up in love.
>
> PASTOR CHUCK SMITH

12. What instructions does Paul give in Philippians 2:3–4?

13. What are some practical things you can do to fulfill this instruction?

14. According to Romans 14:20, what is at risk of being destroyed if we as Christians focus too much on the temporal, or physical, realm?

15. Explain in practical terms how the above destruction could be possible.

16. What is the motivating factor behind Romans 14:21?

17. If the only reason for you to stop a certain behavior was to keep a brother from stumbling, would that be enough to motivate you to stop?

18. How are we to exercise our liberties, based on Romans 14:22?

19. How are we to have faith? What does this mean?

> Without faith it is impossible to please Him, for he who comes to God must believe that He is, and that He is a rewarder of those who diligently seek Him.
>
> HEBREWS 11:6

20. If our actions are not a result of faith, what does Romans 14:23 tell us they are a result of?

Day 5: Review of Romans 14:1–23

Prayerfully read Romans 14:1-23.

Observe, Interpret, Apply
1. Oftentimes Christians debate over what they can do within the boundaries of their liberty in Christ. But as Romans 14 makes clear, instead of seeking what we can get away with, we should seek to please God.

While God gives each of us a free will to do as we please, He has given us guidelines in His Word regarding our actions. But the Bible doesn't specifically call out each possible behavior, and this leaves many so-called gray areas for conduct. Today we will look at a few questions that can help us determine whether the gray areas in our personal lives are pleasing to God or not.

Think of a gray area of behavior you may have had questions about in your own life, such as drinking alcohol, watching movies, listening to certain kinds of music, or wearing particular types of clothing. Ask yourself the following questions to help you see God's position on this behavior.

Does Scripture condone or condemn it?

How would this affect my witness for Christ if others knew I was doing it?

Is it spiritually profitable for me to be doing this?

Is there a chance that it could have control over me, if not now, then in the future?

Is it something I would want to be doing when Christ returns?

Does it glorify God?

Does it hurt anyone else?

_____

_____

Could I take Jesus with me to do this?

_____

_____

2. What other questions could help filter your decisions? List them below.

_____

_____

_____

_____

_____

3. Has God shown you that you have compromised your walk with Him in any area of your life? Spend some time in prayer, asking Him to search your heart to see if there is any wicked way in you (see Ps. 139:24). Write a prayer thanking Him for His provision of grace to enable you to do what only He can empower you to do.

_____

_____

_____

_____

_____

4. Below are a few scriptures to encourage you to draw closer to God. Finish your study today by meditating on these scriptures and allowing God to speak to your heart.

Psalm 119 (especially 119:9, 11):

_____

_____

_____

Draw near to God
and He will
draw near to you.

JAMES 4:8

John 15:4–7:

Colossians 2:6–7:

2 Timothy 2:20–22:

Romans 15:1–33

Others, Lord, yes, others, let this my motto be.
Help me to live for others, that I may live like Thee.

CHARLES D. MEIGS

Day 1: Overview of Romans 15:1–33

Prayerfully read Romans 15:1–33.

In Romans 15 Paul continues the theme of Romans 14, emphasizing the ministry of believers. He begins Romans 15 with the ministry we as believers have toward one another. He uses Jesus as our example in ministry and cites God's Word and prayer as the power for ministry.

Observe, Interpret, Apply

1. As you read over Romans 15, note the divisions in the chart below, and write down key words and phrases to summarize what Paul says about ministry. Then write a chapter title or summary statement for Romans 15.

Romans 15:1–7	Romans 15:8–16	Romans 15:17–33

| | | |
| | | |

Chapter Title or Summary Statement

2. Paul describes God as "the God of" several things. As you read through Romans 15, look for this phrase, and record your findings below.

Romans 15:5:

Romans 15:13:

Romans 15:33:

_____

_____

_____

3. Which of these attributes ministers to your heart most, and why?

_____

_____

_____

Blessed be the LORD God of Israel from everlasting to everlasting! And let all the people say, "Amen!" Praise the LORD!

PSALM 106:48

Day 2: Romans 15:1–7

Prayerfully read Romans 15:1-7.

Observe, Interpret, Apply

1. How are we to bear with one another, based on Romans 15:1-2?

_____

_____

_____

2. Is Paul telling us to be people pleasers? Explain.

_____

_____

_____

3. Compare Romans 15:1-2 with Galatians 1:10.

_____

_____

_____

4. Who does Romans 15:3 say is our example?

> Finally, my brethren, rejoice in the Lord. For me to write the same things to you is not tedious, but for you it is safe.
>
> PHILIPPIANS 3:1

5. What additional information on this subject does Philippians 2:5–9 reveal?

6. What are two reasons that God gave us Scripture, according to Romans 15:4?

7. Read Romans 15:5–7. Who enables us to glorify God?

8. Based on Romans 15:5, in what way can we glorify God?

9. What command is given in Romans 15:7?

10. How does Christ receive us? (See John 6:37.)

_____

_____

_____

_____

_____

11. How can we demonstrate that we are Christ's disciples? (See John 13:34–35.)

_____

_____

_____

_____

_____

We should strive for unity of mind and heart, receiving one another and accepting our differences within the body of Christ. Differences do exist, but they need not divide us into splinter groups. We can accept one another in love, because Christ has received us all. This accepting love marks true spiritual maturity.

PASTOR CHUCK SMITH

Day 3: Romans 15:8–16

Prayerfully read Romans 15:8-16.

Observe, Interpret, Apply

1. Paul quotes from the Old Testament in Romans 15:9–12. Look up and write out the Old Testament scripture that correlates with each quote in Romans 15, and answer each question in the right column.

Verse from Romans	Verse from the Old Testament
Romans 15:9: "For this reason I will confess to You among the Gentiles, and sing to Your name."	Psalm 18:49: What are we called to do?

Romans 15:10: "Rejoice, O Gentiles, with His people!"	Deuteronomy 32:43: What will God do for His people?
Romans 15:11: "Praise the LORD, all you Gentiles! Laud Him, all you peoples!"	Psalm 117:1: What are we called to do?
Romans 15:12: "There shall be a root of Jesse; and He who shall rise to reign over the Gentiles, in Him the Gentiles shall hope."	Isaiah 11:10: What will God do for the Gentiles?

2. According to the quote from Isaiah in Romans 15:12, to whom does the "root of Jesse" refer? Look up the following verses to help answer this question.

Isaiah 11:1–2:

Revelation 22:16–17:

3. In Romans 15:13 Paul calls God the "God of hope." What is our hope?

4. Underline the key words in Romans 15:13 below that show how we abound in hope.

May the God of hope fill you with all joy and peace in believing, that you may abound in hope by the power of the Holy Spirit.

5. Prayerfully look up the following verses, and record what they say about hope.

Romans 5:1–2:

Romans 12:12: Even when we encounter challenging times, what are we to do?

Hebrews 3:6: Who can experience this hope?

6. True hope is only found in Jesus, our eternal hope. Have you been placing your hope in anything less than Jesus? Read 1 Peter 1:3–9, and record your thoughts below. Spend some time in prayer asking God to renew your hope in Him!

_____

_____

_____

_____

_____

> Blessed be the God and
> Father of our Lord Jesus
> Christ, who according
> to His abundant mercy
> has begotten us again
> to a living hope through
> the resurrection of Jesus
> Christ from the dead.
>
> 1 PETER 1:3

7. How does Paul encourage the believers in Rome in Romans 15:14?

_____

_____

_____

_____

_____

8. Of what is Paul "confident," or persuaded, that believers can do for one another?

_____

_____

9. Define "admonish" using your study tools (Strong's #3560), and write its meaning below.

_____

_____

10. All Christians are called to minister to and disciple others, and this includes admonishing. From the following verses, record what you learn about admonishing.

Colossians 1:28–29:

_____

_____

Colossians 3:16:

_____
_____
_____
_____

11. What two things did the grace of God enable Paul to do, according to Romans 15:15–16?

_____
_____
_____
_____
_____

12. Paul was a true minister to God's people, pointing them to the hope that is found only in Jesus. What ministers to you most from Paul's prayer for the church in Romans 15:13–16? Why?

_____
_____
_____
_____
_____

13. Fill in the following acrostic for the word "hope" as it pertains to the ministry we are called to. You can use one word, or you can create a sentence that begins with each letter to spell out the meaning of hope.

H _____
O _____
P _____
E _____

Digging Deeper (Optional)
Define the following words from Romans 15:14.

"Goodness" (Strong's #19):

"Knowledge" (Strong's #1108):

Where do these qualities come from? (See Zech. 4:6.)

Day 4: Romans 15:17–33

Prayerfully read Romans 15:17–33.

Observe, Interpret, Apply
1. What does "therefore" in Romans 15:17 refer to?

2. What did Paul glory in?

3. What did Paul dare not speak of in Romans 15:18?

4. While God calls us all to be ministers of the gospel, who actually does the work of the gospel? (See 1 Cor. 3:6–9.)

5. Why is it vital for a believer to understand and live out this example that Paul set? (See 1 Cor. 4:6–7.)

We have such trust through Christ toward God. Not that we are sufficient of ourselves to think of anything as being from ourselves, but our sufficiency is from God, who also made us sufficient as ministers of the new covenant, not of the letter but of the Spirit; for the letter kills, but the Spirit gives life.

2 CORINTHIANS 3:4–6

6. Those of us who are Gentile Christians must take heed. We have a natural tendency to be proud and self-sufficient before God just like the Jews of the Old Testament were. But just as the Israelite branches were "broken off," so too proud Gentiles will be. According to Romans 15:18, we must keep in mind that all we have received, all we are, and any righteousness we have comes from God as its only source. *There is none righteous, no, not one!*

Do you find yourself boasting in anything or anyone other than what God has done in and through you? If so, confess it before the Lord in writing below, and ask Him to give you the correct perspective.

7. Romans 15:21 is a quote from Isaiah 52:15. Isaiah 52 addresses the Lord's second coming, but in a broader application it refers to evangelism beginning in Paul's day and continuing until Christ's return. Read Isaiah 52:15, and record your findings. Pray and ask God to open your heart to all He has for you.

_____

_____

_____

8. Paul was hindered from going to Rome until he had completed the work God sent him to do: "Now at last I am through with my work here, and I am ready to come after all these long years of waiting" (Rom. 15:23, TLB). This portion of Scripture is a remarkable description of the ministry of God's messenger. It doesn't matter if you are a preacher, a teacher, or a witnessing believer; the principles of ministry are the same for all believers in Jesus Christ. What has God called you to do?

_____

_____

_____

> Let a man so consider us, as servants of Christ and stewards of the mysteries of God. Moreover it is required in stewards that one be found faithful.
>
> 1 CORINTHIANS 4:1-2

9. Could you be more faithful in the work God has put before you? If so, write a prayer asking Him to fill you with His Spirit and enable you.

_____

_____

_____

_____

_____

10. After going to Jerusalem to minister to the saints (see Rom. 15:25), what does Romans 15:24 tell us Paul hoped for?

_____

_____

_____

11. Paul says that "it pleased those from Macedonia and Achaia to make a certain contribution for the poor among the saints who are in Jerusalem" (Rom. 15:26). What was the duty of the Gentile believers mentioned in Romans 15:27?

12. Why was this a duty?

13. According to Romans 15:30, what two sources did Paul use in his "begging"?

14. What did Paul beg the brothers for?

15. Often we feel uncomfortable asking for prayer for ourselves. How does Paul encourage us to seek prayer from others when we are seeking God's will?

16. Look up the following verses, and note the writers' prayer requests.

Ephesians 6:19–20:

> Disunity and disagreement do not glorify God; they rob Him of glory. . . . Receive one another; edify one another; and please one another . . . all to the glory of God.
>
> WARREN WIERSBE

2 Thessalonians 3:1:

Hebrews 13:18:

17. What did Jesus pray for in John 17:20–23?

Digging Deeper (Optional)
Look up in your study tools the following words from Romans 15:30. Write their definitions below.

"Beg," or "beseech" (Strong's #3870):

"Strive together" (Strong's #4865):

_____

_____

_____

_____

> As iron sharpens iron,
> so a man sharpens the
> countenance of his friend.
>
> PROVERBS 27:17

Day 5: Review of Romans 15:1–33

Prayerfully read Romans 15:1–33.

Observe, Interpret, Apply

1. Throughout Romans 15 Paul points to unity. Read the following passages of Scripture, and summarize the key points about unity.

   1 Corinthians 1:10: What was Paul's plea to the body of Christ?

   _____

   _____

   _____

   1 Peter 3:8–9: What was Peter's exhortation to the body of Christ?

   _____

   _____

   _____

2. From Hebrews 10:24–25, comment on three practical ways we are to exhibit unity.

_____

_____

_____

_____

3. God has not called us to be spiritual "fruit inspectors" and pick one another apart. When we see a brother or sister in Christ beginning to drift

away from God, however, we are called to hold one another accountable. What three instructions does Galatians 6:1–2 give to those "who are spiritual" as to how we are to restore a brother or sister in Christ?

4. From Romans 15 and other scriptures below, paraphrase the insights you gained from your study this week about the following topics.

> May the God of hope fill you with all joy and peace in believing, that you may abound in hope by the power of the Holy Spirit.
>
> ROMANS 15:13

Romans 15:1–2: Ministry to weaker believers:

Romans 15:3, 8: Ministry of Jesus:

Romans 15:9–12: Ministry to the Gentiles:

Romans 15:15–29: Paul's ministry:

Romans 15:5–6, 13, 30–33: Ministry of prayer:

1 Timothy 5:8; Ephesians 6:4: Ministry to family:

5. In what way has God called you to minister to the following people?

Believers:

Unbelievers:

Leadership:

Jesus:

When the Spirit of God is freely operating among a company of believers, when the eyes of all of them, first are toward Christ Jesus, they are thinking of Him, of His love, of His service, and of what will please Him. Then follows, naturally, patient dealing with one another, comforting one another. Some of the company may know much more truth than others; many may hold varying judgments or opinions concerning particular matters. But this does not at all touch their unity . . . their conscious unity, in Christ, and it does not in the slightest degree hinder their being of one mind, and working together with one accord, and, in the vivid words of Scripture, being with one mind together according to Jesus Christ.

WILLIAM R. NEWELL

Romans 16:1–27

*God desires to bless us, but we must meet His conditions for receiving blessings.
By staying separate from the world and keeping saturated in the Word,
we may expect God's blessings. Resolve to meditate on the Word of God and obey it.
He will make you a blessing to others.*

WARREN WIERSBE

Day 1: Overview of Romans 16:1–27

Prayerfully read Romans 16:1-27.

One of the overriding themes in Romans 15 was unity in the body of Christ. Now here in Romans 16, Paul provides us brief insight into his personal relationships with many of the believers in Rome. He warns the believers against those who would bring division to the church, names his companions, and concludes his epistle with a blessing.

Observe, Interpret, Apply
1. As you read Romans 16, look for any warnings, admonitions, or commands. Record your findings in the chart below, and write a summary statement about what you learned.

Warnings	Admonitions or Exhortations	Commands

Summary Statement

2. Ask the Lord to give you a greater appreciation for those in the body of Christ. List below some of the Christians you are thankful for as well as what they do for the gospel of Jesus in building the family of God.

_____

_____

_____

_____

_____

Day 2: Romans 16:1–16

Prayerfully read Romans 16:1-16.

Proverbs 18:1 tells us that a person "who isolates himself seeks his own desire; he rages against all wise judgment." As believers in Jesus, we need the family of God. Only in the community of believers can we truly discover the full person of God and His blessings. Community also provides us with accountability, protection from false doctrine, and a sense of belonging.

Romans 16 makes it clear that Paul appreciated and realized the need for other believers. Not only does he greet twenty-six people by name, he also mentions nine of his traveling companions. Let's spend some time today looking at a few of them.

Observe, Interpret, Apply

1. In Romans 16:1–2 Paul makes mention of Phoebe. Her name means "bright, pure, radiant, to shine forth." Phoebe is said to have been a widow from Cenchrea who reportedly traveled from Corinth to Rome to deliver Paul's letter to the Romans. How does Paul describe Phoebe?

I also, after I heard of your faith in the Lord Jesus and your love for all the saints, do not cease to give thanks for you, making mention of you in my prayers: that the God of our Lord Jesus Christ, the Father of glory, may give to you the spirit of wisdom and revelation in the knowledge of Him, the eyes of your understanding being enlightened; that you may know what is the hope of His calling, what are the riches of the glory of His inheritance in the saints, and what is the exceeding greatness of His power toward us who believe, according to the working of His mighty power which He worked in Christ when He raised Him from the dead and seated Him at His right hand in the heavenly places, far above all principality and power and might and dominion, and every name that is named, not only in this age but also in that which is to come. And He put all things under His feet, and gave Him to be head over all things to the church, which is His body, the fullness of Him who fills all in all.

EPHESIANS 1:15-23

2. Using your study tools, look up the following words that Paul uses to describe Phoebe or give instructions regarding her, and write their definitions below.

"Servant" (Strong's #1249):

"Helper" (Strong's #4368):

"Assist" (Strong's #3936):

3. What new insight have you gained from studying Phoebe?

4. In Romans 16:3–5 Paul mentions Priscilla and Aquila. What phrase did Paul use in verse 3 to describe them?

5. What do you learn about Priscilla and Aquila in Romans 16:4–5?

6. What additional information do we find about these two in Acts 18:1-4?

7. How would you characterize Priscilla and Aquila from what you have read? Can the same things be said of you? If not, pray that God would enable you by His grace to serve as they did.

Since we are receiving a kingdom which cannot be shaken, let us have grace, by which we may serve God acceptably with reverence and godly fear.

HEBREWS 12:28

8. How does Romans 16:16 say we are to greet one another?

9. What does this mean? What does it not mean?

10. What do think would happen if the body of Christ today had the kind of loving commitment toward one another that was modeled among the believers Paul mentions in Romans 16?

Digging Deeper (Optional)

List below the attributes or description of Paul's companions as recorded in Romans 16:1–14.

> Behold, how good
> and how pleasant it is
> for brethren to dwell
> together in unity! It is like
> the precious oil upon the
> head, running down on
> the beard, the beard of
> Aaron, running down on
> the edge of his garments.
> It is like the dew of
> Hermon, descending
> upon the mountains
> of Zion; for there the
> LORD commanded the
> blessing—life forevermore.
>
> PSALM 133:1–3

Epaenetus:

Mary:

Andronicus and Junia:

Amplias:

Urbanus and Stachys:

Apelles and the household of Aristobulus:

Herodion and the household of Narcissus:

Tryphena and Tryphosa:

Persis:

Rufus:

Asyncritus, Phlegon, Hermas, Patrobas, Hermes, and the brethren who were with them:

Day 3: Romans 16:17–20

Prayerfully read Romans 16:17–20.

There is no doubt that Scripture calls the body of Christ to unity and love toward one another. There is a condition, however: true unity can be built only when believers embrace the essentials of the gospel. Paul now warns the church that not everyone is there to edify or build up.

Observe, Interpret, Apply

1. What does Paul "urge," or beg, the brethren to do in Romans 16:17?

2. Define the following words using your study tools, and write their meanings below.

"Note," or "mark" (KJV) (Strong's #4648):

"Divisions" (Strong's #1370):

"Offenses" (Strong's #4625):

"Avoid" (Strong's #1578):

3. What do you learn about deceivers in the following verses?

Colossians 2:8:

2 Peter 2:1–3:

Jude 1:16–19:

4. What does Jude call the body of Christ to do in Jude 1:20-22?

5. False teachers and those who cause division should not take us by surprise. Record below what Paul says in 2 Timothy 3:1-9.

6. Of false teachers and divisive people, Pastor Chuck Smith said,

> In the middle of these personal greetings to all his dear friends in Rome, Paul gave a reminder to "note those who cause divisions and offenses, contrary to the doctrines which you learned, and avoid them." In other words, "Stay away from divisive people." I have met many Christians who seem to relish causing division. Some of the first things you notice about them is their lack of love and their constant judging of others. They condemn anyone who doesn't

agree perfectly with their theological perspective. Make a note of those kinds of people and stay away from them. Don't listen to them, because their critical attitude can rub off on you. Let love be your rule of conduct.[1]

According to Romans 16:17, we are to avoid those who teach false doctrines or cause division in the church. What does Paul say in Romans 16:18 is the reason people bring in divisions and false teachings?

7. In Philippians 3:17–20 we see a contrast. List below what you learn about the two kinds of people mentioned in this passage.

Enemies of the Cross	Brethren

8. Just as we see a contrast between those who choose to edify the body and those who desire to tear it down, so too we see a contrast between people according to which god they serve. Jesus says, "You are either for Me or against Me" (see Matt. 12:30). What does Matthew 6:24 say about this?

9. Paul commends the believers in Rome for their obedience. How does Paul exhort them in Romans 16:19?

10. According to the first part of Romans 16:20, what will be the result if we heed Paul's exhortation?

11. We see a familiar phrase in the last part of Romans 16:20; what does Paul call God?

12. How do the following verses help you understand how to experience Christ's victory every day?

Romans 6:11-13:

1 Corinthians 10:13:

_____

_____

_____

James 4:7–10:

_____

_____

Day 4: Romans 16:21–27

Prayerfully read Romans 16:21-27. In the beginning of Romans 16, Paul told the church whom to greet. Now in verses 21-23, Paul greets the church on behalf of his friends and coworkers.

This I pray, that your love may abound still more and more in knowledge and all discernment, that you may approve the things that are excellent, that you may be sincere and without offense till the day of Christ, being filled with the fruits of righteousness which are by Jesus Christ, to the glory and praise of God.

PHILIPPIANS 1:9-11

Observe, Interpret, Apply

1. From Romans 16:21-23, note the qualities or position of each person listed below.

Timothy:

_____

_____

_____

Lucius, Jason, and Sosipater:

_____

_____

_____

Tertius:

_____

_____

_____

Gaius:

Erastus:

Quartus:

2. In Romans 16:25–27 Paul pronounces a benediction (blessing) upon the church at Rome. According to Romans 16:25, what is God able to do for us?

3. Define "establish" (Strong's #4741) using your study tools, and write its meaning below.

The grace of our Lord Jesus Christ be with you all. Amen.

ROMANS 16:24

4. How are you established?

5. How does this encourage you to press into Jesus and know Him more?

6. How are we further established, according to the following scriptures?

Acts 20:32:

1 Peter 5:10–11:

1 Thessalonians 3:12–13:

7. What is the mystery Paul speaks of in Romans 16:25? Refer to lesson 13, day 4 for the definition of the word "mystery" (Strong's #3466).

8. How was the mystery made manifest, according to Romans 16:25–26?

9. What information does Paul give about the mystery? (See Col. 1:26–27.)

10. How widespread does Romans 16:26 tell us the gospel is?

> To Him who is able to keep you from stumbling, and to present you faultless before the presence of His glory with exceeding joy, to God our Savior, who alone is wise, be glory and majesty, dominion and power, both now and forever. Amen.
>
> JUDE 1:24–25

11. How does Paul describe God in Romans 16:27?

12. According to Romans 16:27, through whom is glory given?

Day 5: Review of the Book of Romans

As you review the book of Romans, be refreshed as you think upon all you have studied.

Observe, Interpret, Apply

1. Fill in the appropriate verse reference next to each scripture listed below (all scriptures are from the NKJV):

Romans 1:_____: "Through Him [Jesus] we have received grace and apostleship for obedience to the faith among all nations for His name."

Romans 1:_____: "For in it the righteousness of God is revealed from faith to faith; as it is written, 'The just shall live by faith.'"

Romans 2:_____: "Or do you despise the riches of His goodness, forbearance, and longsuffering, not knowing that the goodness of God leads you to repentance?"

Romans 2:_____: "But he is a Jew who is one inwardly; and circumcision is that of the heart, in the Spirit, not in the letter; whose praise is not from men but from God."

Romans 3:_____ – _____: "As it is written: 'There is none righteous, no, not one; there is none who understands; there is none who seeks after God.'"

Romans 3:_____: "Whom God set forth as a propitiation by His blood, through faith, to demonstrate His righteousness, because in His forbearance God had passed over the sins that were previously committed."

Romans 4:_____: "Now to him who works, the wages are not counted as grace but as debt."

Romans 4:_____: "[Jesus] was delivered up because of our offenses, and was raised because of our justification."

Romans 5:_____ – _____: "Therefore, having been justified by faith, we have peace with God through our Lord Jesus Christ, through whom also we have access by faith into this grace in which we stand, and rejoice in hope of the glory of God."

Romans 5:_____: "Therefore, as through one man's offense judgment came to all men, resulting in condemnation, even so through one Man's righteous act the free gift came to all men, resulting in justification of life."

Romans 6:_____: "Knowing this, that our old man was crucified with Him, that the body of sin might be done away with, that we should no longer be slaves of sin."

Romans 6:_____: "For sin shall not have dominion over you, for you are not under law but under grace."

Romans 6:_____: "For the wages of sin is death, but the gift of God is eternal life in Christ Jesus our Lord."

Romans 7:_____: "But now we have been delivered from the law, having died to what we were held by, so that we should serve in the newness of the Spirit and not in the oldness of the letter."

Romans 7:_____: "O wretched man that I am! Who will deliver me from this body of death?"

Romans 8:_____-_____: "There is therefore now no condemnation to those who are in Christ Jesus, who do not walk according to the flesh, but according to the Spirit. For the law of the Spirit of life in Christ Jesus has made me free from the law of sin and death."

Romans 8:_____-_____: "For I am persuaded that neither death nor life, nor angels nor principalities nor powers, nor things present nor things to come, nor height nor depth, nor any other created thing, shall be able to separate us from the love of God which is in Christ Jesus our Lord."

Romans 9:_____: "For He says to Moses, 'I will have mercy on whomever I will have mercy, and I will have compassion on whomever I will have compassion.'"

Romans 9:_____: "But indeed, O man, who are you to reply against God? Will the thing formed say to him who formed it, 'Why have you made me like this?'"

Romans 10:_____: "For Christ is the end of the law for righteousness to everyone who believes."

Romans 10:_____-_____: "If you confess with your mouth the Lord Jesus and believe in your heart that God has raised Him from the dead, you will be saved. For with the heart one believes unto righteousness, and with the mouth confession is made unto salvation."

Romans 10:_____: "So then faith comes by hearing, and hearing by the word of God."

Romans 11:_____: "And if by grace, then it is no longer of works; otherwise grace is no longer grace. But if it is of works, it is no longer grace; otherwise work is no longer work."

Romans 11:_____: "For of Him and through Him and to Him are all things, to whom be glory forever. Amen."

Romans 12:_____-_____: "I beseech you therefore, brethren, by the mercies of God, that you present your bodies a living sacrifice, holy, acceptable to God, which is your reasonable service. And do not be conformed to this world, but be transformed by the renewing of your mind, that you may prove what is that good and acceptable and perfect will of God."

Romans 12:_____: "Be of the same mind toward one another. Do not set your mind on high things, but associate with the humble. Do not be wise in your own opinion."

Romans 13:_____: "And do this, knowing the time, that now it is high time to awake out of sleep; for now our salvation is nearer than when we first believed."

Romans 13:_____: "But put on the Lord Jesus Christ, and make no provision for the flesh, to fulfill its lusts."

Romans 14:_____: "Who are you to judge another's servant? To his own master he stands or falls. Indeed, he will be made to stand, for God is able to make him stand."

Romans 14:_____: "It is good neither to eat meat nor drink wine nor do anything by which your brother stumbles or is offended or is made weak."

Romans 15:_____–_____: "Now may the God of patience and comfort grant you to be like-minded toward one another, according to Christ Jesus, that you may with one mind and one mouth glorify the God and Father of our Lord Jesus Christ."

Romans 15:_____: "For I will not dare to speak of any of those things which Christ has not accomplished through me, in word and deed, to make the Gentiles obedient."

Romans 16:_____: "Now I urge you, brethren, note those who cause divisions and offenses, contrary to the doctrine which you learned, and avoid them."

Romans 16:_____: "For your obedience has become known to all. Therefore I am glad on your behalf; but I want you to be wise in what is good, and simple concerning evil."

Romans 16:_____: "The grace of our Lord Jesus Christ be with you all. Amen."

Now to you who have completed this study, I say, "Well done, good and faithful servant. . . . Enter into the joy of your Lord" (Matt. 25:21).

Notes

Introduction: How to Study the Bible

1. *Biblesoft's New Exhaustive Strong's Numbers and Concordance with Expanded Greek-Hebrew Dictionary,* Bible software (Biblesoft and International Bible Translators, 1994).

2. Spiros Zodhiates, *The Complete Word Study Dictionary: New Testament* (Chattanooga: AMG, 1993), 771.

3. *Nelson's Illustrated Bible Dictionary,* PC study Bible (Nashville: Thomas Nelson, 1986).

Lesson 2: Romans 1:18–32

1. Thoughts in question 7 adapted from Brian Brodersen, "Answers for a Post-Christian Culture," Calvary Chapel Pastors' Conference Archives, https://calvarychapel.com/resources/article]view/answers-for-a-post-christian-culture/ (accessed July 3, 2017).

Lesson 3: Romans 2:1–29

1. Warren Wiersbe, *Be Right: How to Be Right with God, Yourself, and Others,* Be Series Commentary: Romans (Wheaton, IL: Victor, 1977), 7.

Lesson 4: Romans 3:1–31

1. *Biblesoft's New Exhaustive Strong's,* Bible software.

Lesson 6: Romans 5:1–21

1. *Nelson's Illustrated Bible Dictionary,* PC study Bible.

Lesson 8: Romans 7:1–25

1. Ruth Paxson, *Life on the Highest Plane,* vol. 1, "The Person and Work of Christ," chap. 1, "Human Life on Three Planes."

Lesson 12: Romans 10:1–21

1. Chuck Smith, The Word For Today Bible (Nashville: Thomas Nelson, 2006).

Lesson 14: Romans 12:1–21

1. Chuck Smith, *The Gospel According to Grace: A Clear Commentary on the Book of Romans* (Costa Mesa, CA: Word for Today, 2007).

Lesson 18: Romans 16:1–27

1. Smith, The Word for Today Bible, 1491.